Praise for Sharon Tate and the Daughters of Joy

Sharon Tate and the Daughters of Joy is like watching academia and history being blown to pieces with a pop-culture shotgun. Herrle combines known elements in new forms, turning his prose into the literary version of an M.C. Escher lithograph. This is a witty, wildly imaginative and very ballsy homage to all things estrogen.

— Gabino Iglesias, *Verbicide* magazine

Herrle plays his words like jazz, refusing to follow the most traveled way. His intellect, rather than intimidating readers, draws us in and invites . . . Then there are the swirls of intensity that force the reader into places that might reflect too much truth: the essence of worthwhile poetry.

— Ward Abel, author of *Cousins Over Colder Fields* and member of the band Abel, Rawls & Hayes

I felt like Scrooge being led by the specters: the changing of the guides, scenes of time and place, and mix of poetry and prose. Herrle paints using whatever he deems necessary — literature, history, science, art, nature — masterfully balancing the vile and debauched with the beautiful. [A] work of blinding brilliance.

— Jennifer Perry, creator of *Madame Perry's Salon*, and owner of Lone Wolf Communications, LLC

Profound and exquisite . . . the musings of a vast intelligent brow that scales the dark cupboard shelves of time in pursuit of a rationale for the death of beauty . . . expounded through a thousand historical and pop cultural references . . . prefer[ring] "Zorro black" over the Pimpernel's scarlet. It's been some time since [I've been] so inspired by poetry.

— David Gough, painter and creator of *Man/Son and the Haunting of the American Madonna*

A brave literary contribution.

— Jane Freese, librarian and author of *In Madera Canyon*

SHARON TATE AND THE DAUGHTERS OF JOY

BOOKS BY DAVID HERRLE

Poetry

Sharon Tate and the Daughters of Joy   (2013)

Abyssinia, Jill Rush   (2010)

SHARON TATE AND THE DAUGHTERS OF JOY

DAVID HERRLE

Time Being BookS
An imprint of Time Being Press
St. Louis, Missouri

Time Being Books
10411 Clayton Road
St. Louis, Missouri 63131

Time Being Books® is an imprint of Time Being Press®, St. Louis, Missouri.

Time Being Press® is a 501(c)(3) not-for-profit corporation.

Time Being Books® volumes are printed on acid-free paper.

ISBN 978-1-56809-222-5 (paperback)

Library of Congress Cataloging-in-Publication Data:

Herrle, David, author.
  [Poems. Selections]
  Sharon Tate and the Daughters of Joy : / David Herrle. — First edition.
    pages cm
  ISBN 978-1-56809-222-5 (pbk. : acid-free paper)
  I. Title.
  PS3608.E7758A6 2013
  811'.6—dc23

                                                              2013046534

Cover design by Jeff Hirsch
Cover art, "The Valley," by David Van Gough
Book design and typesetting by Trilogy M. Mattson

Manufactured in the United States of America
First Edition, first printing (2013)

ACKNOWLEDGMENTS

Thanks to my wife for keeping a light in the window while I toured hell.

Thanks to artist David Gough for offering *The Valley* as the cover image and engaging in insightful discussions about the Manson era and bloody history in general. Please visit his www.davidgoughart.com and http://davidgoughart.blogspot.com.

Thanks to brilliant Professor Don "Tex" Taylor, who inspired my enduring respect for and insight into history. You're the good Tex, sir.

Thanks to my grandfather. I thought he'd live forever — and he did.

CONTENTS

Part 3: Black Dahlia Nihilismus

BENEDICTION

SHARON TATE AND THE DAUGHTERS OF JOY

INVOCATION

This symbol is used to indicate that a stanza has been divided because of pagination.

The Sounds of Names and Dooms

Recite!

Sharon Tate.
Sharon Marie Tate.

Recite!

Queen Antoinette.
Queen Marie Antoinette.

Recite!

Mary Kelly.
Marie Jeanette Kelly.

Say and hear their names!
Sharon Marie Tate, Queen Marie Antoinette, Marie Jeanette.

Sisters in both sound and doom:
Severed by Mansons, Jacobins,
a maniac, Man-Gods.

Recite!

Sharon Tate.
Queen Antoinette.
Mary Jane.
Ladies, live again!

Recite!

Part 1:
Reverse Galatea

Men are such jerks about beautiful women.
— Candice Bergen in *People Weekly* July 28, 1975

To me, beauty is the wonder of wonders. It is only shallow
people who do not judge by appearances.
— Lord Henry, *The Picture of Dorian Gray*

Loveliness unfathomable . . . I look deep down and do believe.
— Starbuck, *Moby-Dick*

A Girl Named Sue

The name Sue underwhelms me. Put some lipstick on it
and make it Susan or even Suzanne, then I'm partly
wooed, for I find deep importance in a female's name,
believe that it predestines her looks-wise, or at least
augurs a cute-proneness, shapes the coming woman
as perpetual water sculpts mountains and hews canyons.

Margarita Carmen Cansino shaped a Rita Hayworth,
a Cleopatra Thea Philopator seduced imperial Rome.
Plain Joan Lucille became platinum Mamie Van Doren,
Lulamae Barnes was dyed and reborn as Holly Golightly.

Charmed names beautify so-so physiques and faces while
fair faces redeem drab or marmish names after the fact,
veto their givens' ominous sonorouslessness or tendency
toward plainness ("Sharon" and Mary" are a dime a dozen
but "Jane" is far from plain) and imprint them as mighty
beasts leave traces on soft land (pre-Marilyn Norma Jean,
singer Harriet Wheeler, painter Whistler's Maud) — like Princess
Margaret and Ann-Margret, unlike poor Margaret Fuller.

Sue Lyon of *Lolita* fame triumphed against heinous Suellyn,
Quixote's "Dulcinea del Toboso" turned a peasant into a queen.
Just one *k* added to "Ivana" birthed the fairer Ivanka Trump,
and cries of "La Esmeralda!" ring to drown Notre Dame's bells.

Augustus, Augustine, Pythagoras, Archimedes, Elvis, David:
these sing to me, but names *glow* only when emasculated,
ovarily sugared, Candy Darlinged and drag-queened by
Aubrey Beardsley — then there are females cross-dressed in
male names (painter Schiele's Wally Neuzil) and abracadabras
that crack clouds when chanted in full bloom: Anais Nin becomes
Angela Anais Juana Antolina Rosa Edelmira Nin y Culmell.

Incant: *Lola Falana, Leonor Fini, Zhang Ziyi, Dree Hemingway, Aaliyah!*
Gina Lollobrigida, Artemisia Gentileshi, Rihanna Fenty, Sussudio!

Familial iterations of gender-neutral "Drew" forged Drew Barrymore.
My anthroponomastic case rests on Dakota Fanning and January Jones.

El Nina

Beauty is a Eurydice.
My sight reaches, misses.

Makes me lonely, drunk.
Strikes low all highs.

Paintings, comic books, couture ad campaigns,
covers of *Vogue*, *Marie Claire*, *W*, *Cosmopolitan*:
impossible oughts, ocular heroin.

You know that throat-lump
just before a good cry?

Every shadow of She hardens
my Adam's apple.

It's not lust, not prurience.
It's heartache, a loss.

I sense her in every bombshell,
in every debutante,
every MILF.

It's this-no-it's-that, almost It,
the veiled Intended,
the veil itself.

Debbie Harry, glisten to me!

My sight reaches, misses!
She slips between blinks.

Can you cup music in your hands?
Can you recite silence?
Can you bell a catastrophe?

She makes everything sad.
I laughweep.

My sight reaches, pleads — "One touch!"

Reverse Galatea, or the Katygorical Imperrytive

Feed Shakespeare's 130th sonnet to the paper shredder!

I stand against genetic egalitarians, insisting — and proving — that there *are* perfect tens among us, that the streets, malls, schools, slums and cubicle lands teem with females that shame Playmates, Dallas Cowboy Cheerleaders, Gibson Girls, Miss USAs.

Physical beauty and limbic dope can't make us righteous or inspire peace (those darling pinups on bomber noses: all *femmes fatales*) so we must abstract delectable flesh into concept, Muse, trickle-up aesthetics: unveil the Sublime, inform the world of Forms.

This is the Reverse Galatea, an unreification, a Cocochanelism. Let's piss off gender-feminists and Left and Right ascetics.

My radical subversion compels me to saturate the social sphere with post-Pre-Raphaelite cream women, hot ebon lovelies and supermodels, conflate proto-Soviet Plato with *Marie Claire*, shine pop culture's flooziest swan-sired Helens into Nurse Ratcheds' eyes.

Offend puritan Hitlers, Marlene Dietrich! Toss your bra at social realism, Dita Teese! Muffle Rembrandt noses, Courbet bushes!

The Aesthetes were right in praising scopophilic and olfactory bondage: arresting style and images, powder, blush and perfume, Prada over *Pravda*, because curative visual frottage stimulates a sugary ooze to gum up utilitarian machines and appall soul-police.

Mary Poppins is Julie Andrews (not the marm of the books), Gypsy Rose Lee frees, Trudy Stein jails, Joplin's a jalopy, and Katy Perry's a Ferrari.

We need gorgeous gargoyles to repel drab demons, a return to pulp magazines' dichotomous depictions: an aesthetic equivalent to war-propaganda art that defends the pure genius of being good-looking. Who's afraid of Naomi Wolf? Not us! Beauty is an ever-expanding box!

Pin-up artists Vargas and MacPherson are high-treasonous. The centerfold is a revolutionary act.

Crave the Craving

for Jacques Lacan

Kant presents the scene of a man
given limitless reign over the woman
of his dream of dreams in any manner
and for however long he can endure —
with a fatal caveat: the man must submit
to the hangman's noose after sweet climax.

Who'd bet that the Pleasure Principle
will urge the man to prefer his neck over
the desire of his little head, heed the gallows'
shadow and cheer his capacity for overcoming
rapacious flesh? It's a no-brainer for the tramp-trumping
brain, survival over desire, a win for socially correct decorum.

However, Dostoyevsky's Underground Man
considered the inconvenient truth that we don't
always choose according to self-preservation, don't
always weigh options in favor of reason: for nonsense
often seems the surest path to acquiring what we crave —
unless the big head cools and considers the scenario carefully,
killing the desire completely, because non-reason is its requisite.

There's another (unsaid, tricky) caveat, horny men:
when we tear back the bed cover to reveal the angel
beneath, there will be a certain uncertain poverty in her
looks, we might even gasp, "Who smuggled in this imposter?"
Or she might sour, taste bad, disgust and repulse us in mid-screw.
Isn't this what happened to poor Jack Torrance in the bathroom
of the Overlook Hotel in *The Shining*: starting with the whore-goddess
and ending up with the cackling hag whose moistness was rot's pus?

"She is what I want!" the man gasps, attacking the hot prize
in exchange for his not-so-dear life. Then: "Wait! That's not her!"
Another woman splays for him and he runs to her, groaning: "Here!
Yes! *Her!*" Then: "No, it's *not* her! Where is *she*? Where?" Then another
woman, another woman, another, another — until the noose itself seems
to be the actual path to the craved thing: "Hang me! Hang me now!"

Poor man, you crave the craving.
Save your neck.

The Eyes Have It, Scopophiles

Is sin in the eye?
Sin seems to be in the eye.
Yes, we sin from the eye.

(Has there ever been a reprehensible blind-from-birth person?)

Seeing is deceiving.
The eye is a lustful berry.
It's the crime scene's nucleus.

Covetousness, sex fantasies,
premeditations, strategies:
rods and cones, electricity.

("The optic nerve made me do it!")

We, the seeing, are in a hall of assaultive
delights, of temptations, of mirrors.
Yes, of mirrors. Vision makes vanity.

They, the blind, are suspended
in a limbo, can't even see darkness,
relegated to describing groped invisible elephants.

For them music is a woman: dense-
score hair, hips' round adagio.
Music, she creates synesthetics.
Her name is Glissando.

Sin is in the eye.
The seen are voyeurs' slaves,
racists' bull's-eyes, rapists' desserts.

We, the guilty, feel the fire.
And we resent those who seem
washed clean by blind waters.

(Innocence is out of sight.)

Hail Snobbism!

Propaganda minister and hack novelist Joe Goebbels
tore art from aesthetes' circles and tossed it like circus
bread to the common man (the Fatherland's "organic
bond"), outlawing critics for their "worm-eaten snobbery"
so that artists could prime the pump with optimistic, folkish
culture freed from wealth's bored decadence and torpor.

The First World's favorite dictator, FDR, democratized art
so that books, films, plays and visual works could address
and edify the common man (the U.S.'s "heart and soul"),
the ordinary workaday world, rather than idle in snooty
galleries and thrill the eyes and ears of only the uncommon.
"Everywhere people are painting, building, writing poetry,
singing and acting" is not from a speech written for FDR but
a boast by true-believer Goebbels, foxy Magda's trollmate.

Homeless bum and art failure Hitler tramped the Vienna streets,
seeking purpose and honor until recruited by one of the biggest
bunch of activist optimists ever to have bruised history: Nazis,
who preached that it takes a village to raise brave new men
and a democratic, nature-sopped art to express "the beautiful
and lofty," the People's "naïve and unbroken joyousness" when
dazzled by the *kitschy* ideal of saccharine landscapes, florals,
wildlife, Spartan men, plain-vanilla and ungussied-up females —
and literally and spiritually lame Goebbels' favorite: *Farmer Venus*.

Poppycock and puritanism!
Art must shine through a cultured prism.
Debbie Harrys must walk angelically among pig-pen punks!
Vogue, voguer, voguest: Save the *haute* from the Folk.

Who Knew I'd Befriend Otto Dix?

As Churchill chose Stalin in lieu of Satan,
I pact with Otto Dix, the Nazi-hated
"degenerate" artist, against Year Zeros
and their propriety, their cultural DDT.

If raunch offends Caesar, let it offend Caesar.
lipstick and rouge against puritan Aryans.

Pour jazz into post-Weimar years' ears,
splash Kandinsky into Nazi prudes' eyes.

Defang Kate Millett with Norman Mailer's pen,
Miss Americanize the gender-feminist.

Let the vulgar nude anger the Inquisitor,
monstrositize when Michelangelo is law.

Rule of Flaw

Why are so many ugly-
duckling stories reiterated?
To condition the children
to suspect every equivalent
to the Barbie doll.

To flaunt blemishes, any
congenital brokenness,
ill proportions, acne, cellulite
anti-*Vitruvian Man* bad postures.

To sledgehammer cathedrals,
gore museums like loose bulls,
behead the homecoming queen
and crown the homely, label all
office babes undeserving bimbos.

There's a thrill in defacing, in
aesthetic vandalism, in ruin,
because natural or cosmetic
beauty blasphemes disorder
and deepens spleen, rebuts
obese and unhygienic excuses.

I know this when I contrast my
own reflection with real Apollos
and Eratos, sniffing back the snorts,
champing at the resentful bit,
aware of the roused rabble inside
that longs to level every visage.

Perfect Imperfection

The desire for perfect 10 is an Icarus,
goes too far up.

We aren't meant for pure heaven any
more than we are for pure earth.

Those wrinkles, that paunch, those sags and freckles,
the Rubens buttocks' indulgent tremors.

Dehanchement (that half-sleepy slur of posture) lures
more than aplomb verticals, linear pageant queens.

The quirks, the unique deviations from Barbie, entice.
Perfect sixes or sevens, lickable asymmetry.

Look closely and you will see that there is
always one eye that excels.

Flight from blemish and frump is wise, but
Photoshops sell overwrought dolls.

Soon the show's over, and the curtain falls.
Age.

I Pay the Toll for Thee, Belle

The dandy and the deformity
are both aesthetes: the former
exuding, the latter osmosing.

There can be a gallant in the monstrous hunchback
and a monster in the groomed gentleman.

Isn't there sympathetic chemistry in "Elephant Man" Merrick?
Isn't Quasimodo the most chivalrous hero?

While many undesirables prefer
to vandalize rather than admire,
some aesthetic cripples dance
for carnal royalty, appreciate
the glow of their genetic betters.

Isn't woman the anti-monster, or, as Maistre
would say, the beautiful animal?

She turns even ogling freaks of nature
into heroic nobles compelled to serve
and protect both queens and molls.

Cover-Girl Soul

I've never been one for Emerson's
Over-Soul, but over and over
again I blunder into a belief
in a Cover-Girl Soul which
redeems eyes that have
seen horrors.

I must remind myself what Issa said:
that flowers enamor our eyes
as we walk on hell's roof —
abyss-devils swim under us,
God help us.

Cover Girl, fragrant Fiction,
your bones will know this
as they recycle in soil
excruciatingly slowly,
vitamining flowers.

I think of Tutsi-women corpses
minced by machetes,
their breasts useless
wastes, their go-
nowhere feet.

I see impossibly motiongenic Sharon
Tate stroll or just sniff her nose with
Martha-Graham gracefulness (her
surely mad-scientist-made mouth
and teeth): now coroner meat.

With the Hunchback I cry: "No blood upon her!"

Who dares to transgress the chivalric law?
These women must live. To mar or
kill these women is to murder
the soul of Man.

Garbo with a Thousand Faces

Kierkegaard wrote that poets are necessary to sing
praises to crucial heroes and transform the sounds
of sorrow and pain into beautiful music with their
verse despite inherent unhappiness.

I take that a step farther: the poet *as* hero, for without
romantic heroes we're doomed to despair and anti-life.
I thrill at the Scarlet Pimpernel protecting his beloved
Marguerite, and I dream of donning Lincoln green when
seeing Errol Flynn's Robin Hood saving de Havilland's Marian.

Sometimes I'm Spider-Man using my web to snatch lady-
love Gwen Stacy away from impending Goblin-spun doom,
or I'm shy Quasimodo harboring my fair La Esmeralda from
men's vampiric lust and the injustice of the gallows noose.

Yes, my fantasy involves both the damsel *and* the hero
swinging away, for I want to delay my due death as well.
Why *should* I want to undergo such an unnatural process?
There's Something Wrong in this world. Its name is Death.

I declare perpetual war against rabid revolutionaries, elusive
Jack the Rippers, Manson's devil's businessmen, guillotine-feeding
and misery-perpetuating humanitarians, and, refusing to drown
in the bloodbath, I aspire to be the time-traveling hero who saves
history's Garbo with a Thousand Faces from the tooth and nail,
masses' tantrums, the very rot of the Reaper.

The Sorcerer's Apparatchik

The disappointed believer and lover of life will
be turned into a cynic and a destroyer.
— Erich Fromm

You ask me what the secret
of mass violence is.
It's beauty.

Resentment or envy of it,
letdowns, spurn-burns.

A fetish for its order without
its "oops" factor.

An unreaching of the high bar,
a falling short.

Rage rages and becomes a ruling stone
when pacifism falls to pieces.

Mountains at molehills' mercy:
dwarfs hack knees.

Dirging depressives demolish
delightful discos.

Wigwams spit grass and sticks
at Frank Lloyd Wright.

The homely surveils the home
of the comely, covets.

Solution?

Punish beauty for its failure to fail,
its contrast of mug shots.

Napoleon the Third strikes Courbet's
Bathers with a whip.

Part 2:
Saint Guillotine

The true cultural revolution would be the reestablisment of monarchistic hierarchies.
— Salvador Dali, *Dali by Dali*

Mock on, Mock on, Voltaire, Rousseau!/Mock on, Mock on — 'tis all in vain!
— William Blake, *Notebook*

[Y]et while I earthly live, the queenly personality lives in me, and feels her royal rights.
— Captain Ahab, *Moby-Dick*

De Sade Slept Here

When the Bastille fell and the mere seven prisoners were freed and the rabble declared open season on the *Ancien Regime*, Marquis de Launay booted Desnot in the balls, so Dezzy used a pocketknife instead of a sword to liberate Launay's head from his royalist neck as a deadly precedent gelled.

That same day, foreskin-challenged King Louis XVI, Bourbon, Mason, coital-coward locksmith and hubby of "Austrian wolf" Antoinette (his key turned lucklessly in her lock for so long), the sun incarnate, clinically depressed Citizen Capet, his reticence his primary sin, wrote one word in his hunting journal:

Rien.
"Nothing."

Team Antoinette

> *I must go like an actress, exhibit myself to a public*
> *that may hiss me.*
> — Marie Antoinette

Thanks to Van Dyke's and Coppola's *Antoinette* films I imagine you as Norma Shearer or Kirsten Dunst: Garbo-rival and gleeful glitterato. I decree these imaginative transmigrations retroactive for every Versailles-curious "lord" and "lady" from 1774 to modernity.

The gulf between your celebrity representative and the looking-glass is always disappointing but that's on you, girl, because when I blow away your Hollywood analogs and blot out the Jacobin harpy caricatures, I see the you of you: the sweet swan of agon.

I place a sword between your royal body and the cannibal public, repudiate the lunatic Republic and stand with my "Austrian whore" in defiance against the knife-swishing fish women and roused rabble who've breached the palace in search of gallons of flowing red justice.

Widow Capet, Earth has gone madder since the Year Zeros in their hubris rebooted Gregory Thirteen's calendar, but, as Manson said, "weeds never die," the head of the Beast is the same, the sermon's still a bore, and demagogic pacifists become bellicose new bosses.

What you've done, corsetless Queen (as did your Romanov soul-sisters Olga, Maria, Anastasia and Alexandra under Bolshevik-devil guns), is absurd: got me to admit monarchical sympathy, to prefer thrones to theses and pray against the Century of the Common Man.

Elle, you are the soap despised by the muck-people, a rain cleansing Woodstock brats and dousing Watts fires, poison versus vermin, Chanel No. 1 against plebeian reek, ice in the house of lava, Snow White among evil dwarfs, my milk and blood, my darling Deficit, my saving Grace.

Charlemagne, Henry Four and the Sun King aren't my Golden Agers, and our Constitution, not nobles or overlords, is the soundest corrective, but I wish *Scarlet Pimpernel*-author Orczy could have written me into your era, my A-Plus, Madame Veto, Ostrich Bitch, my retroactive Dunst: a colorful *pouf* feather floating over the growling, gray Great Fear.

Empress Josephine's Insomnia Explained

Why can't you sleep soundly, sterile Josephine, rose
expert and usurper Napoleon's soon-divorced empress?
Why can't your pretty head rest on Tuileries pillows?
What, in all this Revolution-given glory, queers your dreams?

"I can feel the Queen's ghost asking what I am doing in her bed."

This Is What Democracy Looks Like,
Princess de Lamballe

Your existence
contrasts
envious sheep
in wolves'
skins.

They demand
your head, blonde
beast dressed
in criminal
sequins.

Raped pre- or
post-mortem,
or both, with
or without
your tits.

They rip open
your noble
body, pull the
saucy organic
pasta from it.

Some say a
cannibal
stole your
heart for
a treat.

What righteous
ecstasy froths as
your life gushes
from that Phrygian
-red faucet!

Even de Sade
paled at your
end, your life
the flipside of
his *Juliette* smut.

Rise, Antoinette! Rise, Antoinette!

Madame de Stael (a.k.a. "A Woman") defended the doomed Queen in *Reflections on the Trial of a Queen* thus: "The destiny of Marie Antoinette contains everything that might touch your heart." Baron d'Oberkirch praised: "She is a flame!" And Madame Tussaud said that the Queen's smile could enchant even her most brutal enemies — before her most brutal enemies kicked her charm in the teeth and fed her neck to Saint Guillotine: the cruelest and coldest monarch of France ever. Rise, Horace Walpole's "true goddess!" Rise, Antoinette, and behead these headhunters, the intellectual simpletons of these silly salons.

After the rabble stampeded the Bastille, freed seven prisoners and paraded de Launay's piked head, they found that the meat couldn't hold for much longer, so they demanded that Anna Maria Grosholz (the future Madame Tussaud) replace it with a wax one, a more durable trophy — a far, far cry from waxworks Brangelina, Morgan Freeman, Beyonce, Cher and Miley Cyrus — with which to maintain the follyball game's momentum and top the bloodgasm.

The terrified Queen looked down as the *sans-culottes* breached the Tuileries Palace, dismembering anyone in their path, high on that thrill that always returns humans to their regularly scheduled pogroms, and ignited Chicoms' Rectification (live human dissections), "honor" killings, jihad headhunting, the Wonderland murders (could Sherlock Holmes have proved John Holmes' guilt?), the norm of Third World butchery, Lenin's supersession of czarist brutality, dekulakization, the St. Bartholomew's Day and My Lai massacres, the slaughter of Huguenots, the blood-crazed Hutus, antichrist Nazis and Jonestown Flavor-Aid death drinkers, Jim Crow lynchings, the skeleton-filled Year Zero of Pol Pot's Khmer Rouge, Inquisitions, the rape pandemic, Buchenwald's Bitch and 23 thousand dead in one day at Antietam.

Blonde bombshell Princess de Lamballe, former Superintendent of the royal household, bravely returned from England in solidarity with the monarchy, ignoring friend Antoinette's warning against throwing herself "into the mouth of the tiger," only to throw herself into the mouth of the tiger — no, the rabid sewer rat — and become one of the thirteen hundred slaughtered: head cut off (tossed in Anna Grosholz' lap) and limbs hacked ("wrath in death and envy afterwards," as Shakespeare's Brutus said), a pubic-hair mustache adding cherry-on-top shame for this depetalled white dahlia.

Cagliostro, drum up a séance and tell us what's up beyond the grave which fans say you cheated with the Elixir of Life. Tell us, tell us, magus Cagliostro, acquitted Bastille inmate who was revered and compared to tomb-duping Christ by Madame Blavatsky, tell us if you see Antoinette's killers, those self-swallowing snakes, those blind guides and despots of liberty drunk on blood they spilled. Tell us, slickster Cagliostro, do you see the Queen's grand *pouf* that dwarfs her nemeses: the high-on-death men of the Assembly's lowlife Mountain? Rise, Antoinette, rise! Aggravate that grave! Forever live the Queen!

Unchained Malady 1

Uncle of the Gore-ious Revolution, augurous Rousseau, co-sire of Saint Guillotine (with Diderot), forecast a Corsican-born illuminatus who would rock Europe like a hurricane: then came short Bonaparte (Hegel's "world's soul") after the brats of the reset calendar blood-flooded France.

In his delicious *Confessions*, Rousseau told of a courtesan he hired for Supreme Being knows what: scepters should've dropped at her feet, she should've enslaved nobles and royals, but there *must've* been some defect in the divine, worthless slut.

He found it: a mutant nipple on one of her otherwise flawless breasts (not sure if it was the areola or the nub), a genetic fuck-up that turned her from a humble Venus into "a monster, rejected by Nature," a deal breaker, a "blind-nippled" mammarian freak.

The courtesan blushed at his horror and stupid gape and schooled him: "Give up the ladies, and study mathematics."

Unchained Malady 2

Oracular Edmund Burke warned of France's folly in his *Reflections* (which was really a prediction, not a looking back), prompting Tom Paine to rant *The Rights of Man*: Paine who almost fell under Saint Guillotine but for the fantastic grace of his unmiraculous God.

Aside from his political works, Burke spieled on the nature of Beauty, rejecting the notion that it relied on proper proportions of parts, mensuration, utility or fitness — for there are countless examples of irregular, idle, unfit hotties who may be hotter because subpar.

When Apollo's away, Dionysos must play, so France danced in frenzy to Rousseau's blind melody while Burke preferred the Versailles glide, claiming that chivalry had died on the day that ten thousand swords slept in their scabbards instead of leaping out to defend the Queen.

He found beauty in littleness, smoothness, unangularity, delicacy and fair color, so no wonder he thought the Queen a "delightful vision."

Unchained Malady 3

Patriotic Tom Paine, badass of the American Revolution, became
a delegate for the French National Convention and then the Assembly,
and praised the Age of Reason by penning *The Age of Reason*
while he (now an enemy alien) withered in a French prison and
feral fraternals showered in counterrevolutionaries' blood outside.

In his *Sketch for a Historical Picture of the Progress of the Human Mind*,
Marquis de Condorcet, elbow-rubber with Voltaire, gushed about
"the limitless perfectibility of the human species" and human salvation
found in scientific progressivism — while he was being hunted down by
Robespierre's gestapo, before he died in prison awaiting decapitation.

The cheerleaders end up being tackled and raped by the team,
"Eat the rich" people turn each other into Soylent Green.

Unchained Malady 4

Prognostic Orwell's Winston thought that freedom lies in two plus two equals four, but Dostoyevsky's Underground Man taught that man isn't mathematical and that two times two equals death, not life. I say two plus two equals five, equals pi, equals fifty-five!

1984's O'Brien explained the nature of Oceanic power as being "a boot stomping on a human face forever," which describes the berserk French ferals and future cousin Maoists perfectly, for there must be perpetual war and repression to prop dead promises, premises.

There is no warmth or butterflies in Winston's and Julia's trysts because their sex is a revolutionary act and nothing more, even "I love you" is a thing from a ghost past repeated as a granted ingredient, a must-say as foreword to non-supple coupling that's just as machine as Oceania.

Even the most intense, affectionate lovers together in allegiance to a cause, in solidarity against variable x, fall short of true love.

Unchained Malady 5

Precocious Percy Shelley had the intellectual hots for Bill
Godwin, his perfectibilitarian spiritual father, so he ditched
his first wife, Harriet, and courted his mentor's daughter Mary
in order to meld the titles son-in-law, son, protégé, thrall.

On the French Revolution, anarch Godwin gushed that
his "heart beat high," so no wonder this wide-eyed, Bysshe-
tailed boy (and his pocketbook) impressed him: utopian
vim and Jacobin to the brim — versus that Byronic gloom.

While Shel and Mary toured hot spots and mused, pissed on
theism with pagan abandon, reimagined mass revolution
through *Hellas* and meatless Queen Mab, pregnant Harriet
drowned in Hyde Park's Serpentine on the same day Godwin
wrote "H.S. dies" — though her corpse was found a month later.

In an act of poetic just deserts, Percy drowned at sea: a volume
of Aeschylus in one of his pockets and Keats in another.

Marquis de Sade: It's All Good

Virtue.
Oh, *please*, girl!
How can you even swallow that pious pie?
Such fast-food isn't digestible, silly angel.
There are much better concoctions with which
to coat the inside of that hymn-silken throat,
nicer tinctures to anoint your urine (how it
would dew your cloistered sewer, aid we sniffing
connoisseurs flaring our nostrils through barred
windows when your ilk passes by these decrepit walls).

You're perfumed by church incense, courtesan-in-
the-making (oh, odious whiff!): priest-reek,
an olfactory mask over detritus from your
entombed and very dead worm-food Christ
(divinely fragrant with putrescine, butyric acid,
cadaverine — you've *got* to see the Holbein of him!),
but my nose is trained to sniff past the sister act
(plumb the nunnery), past that Vicks Vaporub
and find that "Oh, gee" spot that activates the
whore dormant in the girl: the taint of no return,
when hobby horses bore and daddy issues sublimate.

Goodness?
Aw, naw you di'n't, girl!
What is goodness but constancy — and what
the hell is constant but heaven (pride's foolish fantasy
against the grave's nothingness)? Are *you* constant?
Heed me, babe, be truthful. *Are* you? Nature
herself (who Robespierre calls Supreme Being's true
priest) is perpetually permutative and, as such,
she demands nothing constant but constant flux,
Darwinners and losers: wolves gobble lambs and
brothers slaughter brothers — not to mention the
base proclivities that shock you so, that you call
aberration but I call natural harmony, for who but
Nurse Nature bred our appetites and eager organs?

Eternal reward?
That's the holy water talking!
How could heresy deserve a golden star?
*

Sickly know-it-all and enemy of Nature, do you want
to upset the perfect equilibrium of our nurse, our queen:
up-and-down actions and reactions, the magnificent
tension between vices and virgins, the necessity of
devoured lambs and triumphant wolves?

Ask her, girl, just ask her!
Entreat her to consider the moral laws that
you deadhead disciples claim emulate her very order!
Do you know what our nurse, our queen will do?
Laugh in your saintly face (which we'll *have* to whip
into shame, by the by), call you "idiot" and tell you
that the monster, the savage beast before you (yes, me),
is her most faithful disciple (contrary to our prudish
Emperor imprisoning me for scribbling hardcore porn),
for I serve her with ingenious crimes and pleasant infamies —
breathed into my soul by her, because in her matriarchy
the bigger the profanation, the better, girl.

There.
So, you've no right to complain.
Grin and *bare* it, trainee trollop. Welcome chemical
determinism, lavish agonies, the kiss hidden in every kick,
alignment with the facticity of fact, the rule of scofflaw
that requires a bleating lamb to delight the satyrical wolf.
And when it's all Sade and done (sorry, it's my precious
go-to pun), when you see that every tearful frontier has
been breached, that honor is mere steam from churchy
humours (nothing a little bloodshed won't fix), that religion
is a fart and death is sleep that leaves no wake — you won't
give a *foutre* if you die in my stained and rancid bed or
under that thirsty libertine, the guillotine.

"For Eight Days I Was in Love with Charlotte Corday" *

The Bastille Day parade was cancelled,
but I caught sight of you speeding through
the rues, brewing Plan B, smart Charlotte.

I'd kept an eye on you ever since you arrived
in Paris from Normandy. (You could say I'm
a sucker for Rousseauian-turned-royalist babes.)

You wrote to rat-faced Marat, that ugly, rash-covered
son-of-a-bitch who was yet another doctor turned
executioner (think Mengele, Shiro Ishii, Jonestown's Schacht).

He didn't buy your ruse of sharing Girondist subversives'
names, so you went straight to his pad and demanded
urgency, so he barked an order to let you in.

Soaking in the bathtub to soothe his super acne
or whatever that skin curse was, he was delighted that
you brought more heads for his patron Saint Guillotine.

Like his spiritual cousin Che, he was aroused by yet
another chance to sign death warrants, but you had
one of your own to sign, smart Charlotte.

I watched you pull the five-inch knife from your dress
and sink it into his chest, the carotid artery bawling
ecstatic blood, as if his freak rash had become fluid.
(Paint *that*, sycophant Jacques-Louis David!)

Tribunaled and sentenced, you were led, my Sophie Scholl,
to the scaffold where you said, just before the chop, that
you'd done your duty, that "the rest is nothing."

I was in love with you for eight days, Madame Corday.
Until my head followed yours into the basket.

---

*Written by Pierre Notelet after witnessing Charlotte's execution

Celestial Guillotine

Welcome to the die-land of Doctor Marat, gutters flowing with
rotten blood! Behold the patriot locks of feral ephebe Saint-Just!

Need a "republican shave?" Want to "shake the hot hand?"
Literally lose your head in the rabble's tornadic glee and spit?

Robe, Robe, Robespierre knee-deep in a sanguine Seine,
Mirabeau, Mirabeau, Mirabeau, Mirabeau, all life ends in sleep.

This mighty scaffold is the ultimate Occam's razor, the only answer
to counterrevolutionary questions, another question: "Who's next?"

(150 years later Mao, another gnat-despot, says, "Heads will fall.
Heads will be chopped off, of course, of course.")

Who let the bullshit into the China shop, filled crystals with pig slop?
Monarchs are no bargain, but crustaceans over upper-crust is worse.

Robe, Robe, Robespierre knee-deep in a sanguine Seine,
Mirabeau, Mirabeau, Mirabeau, Mirabeau, all life ends in sleep.

The nerve! Treating Louis and Marie like Mussolini and Clara Pitacci!
Scandal-igniting slut Nicole d'Oliva dares to impersonate Antoinette?

Executioner Sanson led the red-high-heeled Queen to the scaffold.
"I did not do it on purpose," she said when she stepped on his foot.

Robe, Robe, Robespierre knee-deep in a sanguine Seine,
Babeuf, Babeuf, proto-Soviet Babeuf, class war sure cures spleen.

All told, this celestial saint, this glorified cigar cutter, this blind and deaf
monarch with one big tooth, bit through tens of thousands of necks.

Welcome to Celestial Guillotine, Robespierre and unjust Just!
Chins up, Citizens! *Your* turn to stroll down the Queen's last route!

Robe, Robe, Robespierre knee-deep in a sanguine Seine,
Babeuf, Babeuf, proto-Soviet Babeuf, I pray Reason my soul to reap.

The White Rose

As Clemens Brentano sang against Napoleon,
Sophie Scholl and her brother Hans grew
The White Rose Society in Nazified Munich University.

The Rose cried, "Mass murderer," "Cancer, "Demon,"
"Antichrist!" and echoed Schiller, Cicero, Lao-Tzu and Novalis.
It was not a bloom of peace, but a noisy, nagging conscience.

Caught sowing treasonous pamphlets, the arrested Roses
didn't wilt before the Man-God's wrath while facing
Standelheim Prison's hungry guillotine.

Sophie: "What we did will cause waves."
Hans: "Long live freedom!"

(Dear Hans: *Then* what?)

"The Birds Are Flown"

The Royal Family fled for Varennes.
Lafayette: "The birds are flown."
Tom Paine: "Let them go."

The throne is Bourbonless!
King and Queen sped east!
911 call from Varennes!
Cage the harpy in the Tuileries!

Jean-Baptiste Drouet, Sainte-Menehould
Postmaster, "made" the King and blew
the whistle like a good little proto-fascist.

Madame Veto's gone to Montmedy?
The tart dares try to save her head?
911 call from Varennes!
Cage the harpy in the Tuileries!

Antoine Barnave, zealot of the Revolution,
escorted the royals back to Paris, enduring
royally pissed Madame Elisabeth's lecture
on the disorders lying in excessive liberty's wake.

A Citizen has exposed them!
Their necks for this infraction!
911 call from Varennes!
Cage the harpy in the Tuileries!

Soon charmed to the boots by Antoinette,
Barnave fought for the royal couple's lives
and was guillotined for receiving the Queen's
treasonous polyalphabetic substitution ciphers.

She's du Pompadour and du Barry in one body!
A slut dares to sneer at libertie, egalitie, fraternitie?
911 call from Varennes!
Cage the harpy in the Tuileries!

Revolutions

The American one is inarguable
exception (despite its many sins
and the fact that any war is sin).
All the others were bites worse than barks.

J. Adams, Washington and Jay
reprimanded reprisals (sure, S. Adams
later read Shays the Riot Act) while
purges flourished — were the bread
and butter — in others.

Slavery's dissolution was foregone
conclusion, germinated in what
Fred Douglass insisted nullified the
traditional crime: the Constitution,
the Declaration's efflorescence.

American Forefathers: Goliaths self-
demote themselves to slingshot Davids.
Others: eunuchs claim Casanova's
sloppy seconds.

Optimist Jefferson wore rose-speckled
spectacles during his Parisian vocational
vacation, swearing that he'd face stoning
"as a false prophet" if everything went
the way dark Hamilton guessed it would.

Louis XVI to Liancourt: "This is a revolt."
Liancourt to Louis XVI: "No, Sire, it's a
revolution." And thus the term stuck:
an irresistible dialectic, inevitable as
supernovae and storms.

The French Revolution surfed rage and cupidity
(Derrida said they did what they had to do)
while the American one buffered the blood tide,
loved liberty more than hated kings.

When the mass moves on a professed gut-
righteousness, when only in-line hearts are
fit to rule, then all heads must roll, because
*

every in-line ruler knows his own private out-
of-lineness, his secret selfishness, the need for
perpetual Revolution, unethical cleansing.

Nazis, Che-ites, Maoists, Bolsheviks, Khomeiniacs:
it's quite a feat to nostalgize corrupt Weimar,
Batista, the Manchu, Czarism, the Shah.

The Who said, "Meet the new boss, same as
the old boss." Wrong: new bosses are almost
always worse. Then again, as AC/DC rasped,
"Who made who?"

With Washington as god, Toms Jefferson and Paine
cheerleading, and the French-backed American
Revolution still fresh, *who* flicked the dominoes?
(People, we choose our poisons.)

"I am only what lives inside each and every one
of you," Charlie Manson warned. The feral children
we birthed "are running in the streets and they
are coming right at you!"

Upper-class France decried itself and kissed
lower-class ass with hardly a thought
about unmuzzling the dog that would bite
them, tear them limb from limb.

Danton, Robespierre, Saint-Just and the other
Montagnards dressed up and talked like Imperial
Romans and bore the appropriate fruit: a French
Rome, a French Caesar, a glossier absolutism.

Bored youths root for revolution,
a General Will blood transfusion,
while cute girls check their glow
in windows: sexy necks fresh
meat for gallows.

Beneath the Planet of the Jackanapes

Revolutionary France worshipped the atom bomb
a century and a half before it blew its load in New Mexico.

All hail the Bomb Reason!
Goddess! Purity against
the procuress Queen!

White-clad maidens followed a fanatical hymn-singing band, then
Goddess Reason was borne on a throne before the Convention.

All hail the Bomb Reason!
Goddess! Nutrition against
gaunt Notre Dame!

France was a collective woman made immortal and chaste
by a national hymen-reversal, by democidal tantrums.

All hail the Bomb Reason!
Goddess! Unpenetrated
by Cross and crown!

Women hailed Robespierre as a messiah, swooned as
they would for Hitler and his band of winning losers.

All hail the Bomb Reason!
Goddess! Let Royalist blood
drown the fears of your Citizens!

Germanic wombs quartered Third Reich death-broods,
the so-called fairer sex smitten by Death's Heads.

All hail Fuhrer Schicklgruber!
Man-God! You've blessed us
with fields of lebensraum!

Disgruntled Germans gritted their teeth till their gums
bled, hating the Capitalist Jew and his noble prowess.

All hail the egalitarian Aryan Germania!
Devour fat Rothschilds, Bleichroders!
Redistribute the wealth of Nathans!

All hail the leveler of mountains!
Rise, Common Man! Our Aryan sons
will bury Hebrew con men!

In *Moby Dick* the *Pequod*'s carpenter is both builder
and undertaker: creator of life-sustainers and coffins.

All hail the Bomb Reason!
Goddess! With the whirlpooled
ship we gladly go down!

In *Les Miserables*, carpenter plus executioner equals
the bloodthirsty guillotine: concretized law.

All hail the Bomb Reason!
Goddess! Our hearts fill
the skies like Montgolfier balloons!

Progressive Manhattan Project scientists served as regressive
obliterators, doctors allied with illness.

All hail Little Boy and Fat Man!
Kaboom! Your blessed name: Trinity
nuke test, named for a poem by Donne!

Born in the desert Jornada del Muerto ("journey of death"):
the apex of the rise from the apes, the scientific crown.

An obelisk marks how the West was lost.

Freedom Is the Freedom to Say that A+A = 4

A bum loafs on the palace threshold: should we crown
the bum and award him the sword and the purse?

The uppity eunuch dares to tell Don Juan how to get laid,
the toothless crone ridicules the prom queen.

Bloody rages bake in peacenik love-ins and blind ages spill from
Enlightenments. (Consider the Arctic interior of the humanitarian.)

Reason is a gift that can make Man the most irrational beast,
just as both life and urine issue from our ubiquitous genitals.

Reason divorced from spirit is a genius who can't recognize
himself, and spirit without reason dies on the vine.

Purgative bonfires mistake the human heart for paper.
Purges are vanity, egalitarianism is greed.

Radicals breathe easiest when breathless and imagine
through only delirious -isms and -ists.

Reigns of terror are disappointment and broken schemata.
The egalitarian is a bigot against giants, a giant tantrum.

Death-penalty abolitionists decapitated King Louis Capet,
and peacenik hippies ripped through pregnant Sharon Tate.

King Wenceslas, not a rabble rouser, saved the storm-beaten page,
and crazed cannibal masses cry "Bring us flesh!"

Say "Won't" to the General Will (Nazi "Aryans" are communitarians),
despotic democracy and New Deals!

Give me Shakespeare rather than the poor's plight,
you utilitarians who equate Pushkin with pushpins.

Your praxis is a Tilt-A-Whirl, your science is a corpse.
Long live the bourgeois, viva superfluity!

To hell with heaven-on-earthers.
To hell with mathematics.
To hell with equal.

Davidus the Confessor Studies in Scarlet

Lady, you've read Orczy's *Scarlet Pimpernel*, so I ask you:
will you be my Marguerite and give me an excuse to kick
some ass, to bring down heaven and earth to save you?

I'm the real Pimpernel, self-incarnated from the novel:
a Romantic maniac drunk on Howard Pyle, Johnston McCulley,
Walter B. Gibson, pulps and comic books.

The Lord planted me here to save the lost and distressed,
the besieged, broken, dispossessed, the scaffold-bound.
Call me, and I'll sail the *Day Dream* to you.

Like the pimpernel flower, my petals close before bad
weather comes and lock against fanatic fraternity's
requisite exteriority, my prescience provides asylum.

Lady, your history tellers tell tall tales: one about a rouged
and powdered French Revolution, the best of times after
the worst of times, what Wordsworth called a blissful dawn.

But believe me, it was a disembowelment, a demons' day,
nothing more, Marguerite: the detritus of salons packed with
bored and suicidal aristocrats drunk on the commons' spleen.

Why scarlet, a color I despise for its brightness, clarity, severity,
sore-thumbery and discamouflage, rather than prudent Robin-
Hood Lincoln green or Zorro black, The Shadow black, Batman black?

Because I fear that I'm the reverse of the literature: that I tend
to hide in darkness, that I'm actually a foppish dandy and only
an apparent hero, not a pretend coward masking a mask.

So this unlikable and unlikely color argues for my leap of face,
my wild hurdle from theory to action, my self-exile from caution
and disinterest, my bright-red flight into righteous *praxis*, though
I wonder if an artist should become a soldier — or observe and report.

Lady, I am here to behead Saint Guillotine.
Will you be my Marguerite?

Part 3:
Black Dahlia Nihilismus

He had a really dark side. And he traveled that road twenty-four hours a day in his work, just went back and forth between the dark and light.
— Mickey James on Shel Silverstein, *A Boy Named Shel*

Let us be brave with death . . . let us turn it over on every side, and spell out the enigma; let us look at the tomb in advance.
— *The Last Day of a Condemned Man*

Because if it's not love then it's the Bomb that will bring us together.
— The Smiths, "Ask"

Every man is an abyss. You get dizzy looking in.
— Franz, *Woyzeck*

Skinnered Alive

Beyond freedom
and dignity: no
freedom and dignity.

"Good
riddance"
to man
qua
man?

"Like gods!" Hamlet marvels.
Pavlov gasps, "Like dogs!"

B.F. Skinner drowns Thoreau in Walden Two.

Virus Versus Us: The Influenza Pandemic of 1918

The virus was the perfect terrorist,
lovechild of the First World War.
Our sins are boomerangs, mutate,
bite the hands that committed them.

One hundred million souls taken.
The body count sticks in the throat.
It's too big for tears. Dry eyes stare at vast stats.
(Only a gape and a blank remain after cataclysm.)

All I can say is this: Man inseminated
No Man's Land with mustard gas and
trench muck and No Man was born.

Then that bitch biology supersized
speciescide with a mutant super flu:
"You litter my hide with corpses to rats'
delight? *Here's* a donation to your vermin
soup kitchen, scum. Die, humans, die."

It knew the atomic inkling was in us,
it smelled the coming Manhattan Project.
The virus refuses to suffer rivals.

President "Pontius Pilate" Truman

This is the greatest thing in history!
— Truman on the Hiroshima bombing

Carl Sagan, if you're out there cruising the cosmos
in a dandelion seed, put it in high gear and take
a wormhole back to Los Alamos, 1942, just in time
to interrupt the atom bomb's debut Rapid Rupture.

After four-term Executive Orderer FDR fried Tokyo,
gave the go-ahead for atomic holocaust and hired
scientists as Army officers, Oppenheimer helped birth
the Blast that birthed colicky Little Boy and Fat Man.

So hurry, doper astronomer, because we need you
to knock some sense into these cloistered wonks
before they perfect that baloney-destruction kit:
human bodies are baloney, baloney, fried baloney.

"I feel I have blood on my hands," said Oppie to power-
dazzled pipsqueak Truman (oh, you hawk Democrats!):
the Prez whose hands dripped proudly with crimson crude,
who'd chosen "Fini Japs" over conditional surrender.

Find Oppie in his lab or wherever he loafs, tell him what
he can stick in his pipe and smoke while you two quote
the *Bhagavad Gita* or ponder this tragic, Pale Blue Dot.
Anything, anything, but water the Luciferian seed.

Carl, use your gift of gab and school those fools on the cons
and cons of unleashed fission, the morning after scientific
flings, the world-haunting demon, how Marie Curie killed
Karen Silkwood, stand up, adjust that turtleneck and begin:
"We're all sons-of-bitches, earthlings . . ."

The Secret Weapon

Hail the sugar cube!

Something beyond Oppenheimer's
and the Pentagon's vision and expertise,
the secret weapon against Year Zeros.

Egalitarian Caesars: *"Who the hell* needs *sugar in their tea?
Don't you know that the classes clash swords while spoons
stir the drinks of monarchs?"*

Drop one, two, five, ten, twenty cubes
into your tea, ladies! *Plop! Plop! Plop!*
(Take that backjet, envy-louse Pol Pot!)

Dictatorial utopians: *"Tea is the dew of royals! Use the water
for the public laundry or to turn the mill wheel!"*

Flow, tea! Pour, sugar!
Ladies, let your cups overflow!
Sip loudly, rudely!

Gilda

Operation Crossroads at Bikini Atoll,
1946: nuclear bomb tests, one nuke
nicknamed *Gilda*, the other *Helen*.

Were these sinister sisters incarnations
of evil spirits feared by the local
Marshallese, or PETA gods irradiating
crabs to save them from Bikinian bellies?

Evil or altruistic, spirits or gods, at least the nukes
exploded modesty by inspiring the itsy bitsy
teenie weenie weenie-teasing slut bikini,
paving the way for Rita Hayworth covering *Life*,
Annette Funicello — and Godzilla.

Bhagavad Rita

Rita Hayworth,
you sourced
that sexiest
fiction, Gilda,
claiming that
she was figment,
not alter ego.
Couldn't you
have channeled
her to monogamize
Orson Welles, your Shiva?

Deceive us and be
"Love Goddess"
instead of shy lover
and boozer, before
Alzheimer's blows
away your mind
and dignity, stupefies
you from your red font
to your lotus-feet.
What can save you
from the Magic Mirror
Maze and bring you
back from the black velvet?

I incant: *Margaritacansino.*
Cansinomargarita covergirl.
Parvati Hayworth.

I'd love you even
in your derangement
and social disgraces.
Shovel your filth, labor
like Oz to prop the mystery.
This world is an abusive
husband and we're all
sons-of-bitches, Rita,
so spread your tongue
over the battlefield.
Drink our fallen,
shameful
blood.

Count the Sands

Tallying atrocities
is like counting
the sands, says
Erasmus.

Natural selection is
propped by belief in
ghost Progress, in fish
knowing they're wet,
in both having and
eating cake, as if
Nature euthanizes
sickos and saves heroes.

Time plus chance
plus time plus chance
plus time plus chance
doesn't produce
orphanages, courts,
sanctuary, poor boxes.
Non-karmic nature
demands flux and rot.

Only eternity can remedy infinity.

On our own there's no
continuous progress or regress
(though writers are written
upon writers and cities cover
ruins), but there's continuous
tempest: peace-dust vacuumed
by wars, dungeons, the blood-
drenched Colosseum.

Angel/Butcher

Nazi doctor Hans Eisele
was known as "The Angel"
at Sachsenhausen concentration
camp because of his compassion
toward the injured and ailing prisoners.

By the time Hans moved
through Dachau to Buchenwald
"The Butcher" was his nickname,
for his total lack of compassion,
this son of a Lutheran minister.

Artist/Criminal

Jean Genet shares a curiously
similar background with Manson:
unwanted by parents, given
to chronic theft and jail time,
gay prostitution, bitter outcastness.

After migrating from loveless Paris
to Hitler's Germany, why did he
decide to leave the Reich's heart?
Because criminals ruled, so no crime
he'd commit would stand out.

In his works he raised murderers
to hero status and declared crime
the highest beauty. Crime is beauty
and beauty is crime for the self-
despising reincarnabomination-
of-Sade, Nihilnarcissist Genet.

Artist/Bonapartist

Painter Jacques-Louis David
rubbed Max Robespierre's elbows,
apocryphalized proto-Che Marat
and won accolades for his uncool
neoclassicist portraiture and singular
commitment to manifest (perfectly)
dogmatic, political thought.

He served as resident Romanophile
and the Terror's propaganda party
planner, then the Emperor's First Painter
(Napoleon's own interior-decorating Albert Speer).

I can't forgive his deliberately crappy
sketch of condemned Queen Antoinette
awaiting Saint Guillotine's karate chop,
so I imagine Charlotte Corday's ghost
steering the carriage that killed him.

But perhaps his final work was a heart
change, a clue to his realizing that art
mustn't march in army uniforms or sport
Caesar's laurel crown, that feminine nudity
should soften all armor: *Mars Being Disarmed
by Venus and the Three Graces.*

Changed or not, his heart wasn't buried with his body.

Art Doesn't Save

Wagner sang Hitler.
Mao was a poet.

"What an artist
perishes!" boasted
dying Emperor Nero.

Jean-Paul Sartre
mythologized
Che Guevara.

Che transcribed
Pablo Neruda.

"I'm an artist!"
murderer and former
Manson boy Bobby
Beausoleil blubbered
to *SF Weekly*.

What was the name
of the companion plane
for the Hiroshima and
Nagasaki bombings?

The Great Artiste.

Lucid Delirium

When I'm knocking-on-heaven's-door sick,
shivering, whimpering, shitty, delirious,
throat and mouth a riot hose,
I am more lucid than ever.

Though in agony, I savor the trial, lock on to
the clear and present derangement
and remind myself that all is trivia
except good digestion.

From here, outside the wall of dignity, I see
that the forest has no trees, that goals,
worries, acquisition, fatted calves
are biodegradable.

I go down, they go down.
The moon has no light of its own.

What is at the atom's center?
Unstable aperiodic nonlinearity.
Shimmering quanta.
Null-time.
Dream.

Is War This World's God?

Peace? There is no peace!
You say "peace, peace" but there is none.

Strip it of its medals and patches,
salute it with a sneer and a fist,
and rebel-yell that war exists
to feed glutton death — not for
land and kin or incidental moral
goals but to proliferate skeletons,
to glut maggots and engorge vermin
(those surrogate Reaper's mouths).

Repeat the word before a shooting squad:
"Peace peace peace peace peace peace . . ."
It becomes noise, nonsense — noisesense.
And noisesense doesn't stop bullets.

There is a ghoulish lawyer who stands at
the threshold of the door of the War-Law
and negotiates body counts with Jack the
Reaper: "These for those, flesh for these, lives
for this, souls for that, enrich the grave-soil.
Spilled organs like lava, penis-stuffed mouths,
reek and dumb grins of corpses are for you,
our love, for you, our lover, for you, our
widow-maker, our deflowerer."

Say it as they bury you alive: "Peace? Peace?"
Your noisesense doesn't halt the falling soil, melt
executioners' hearts, repel Apocalypse.

Earth bows to Ares, not Cupid, so peace-
makers are the most volatile anarchs.
If the world is patrolled by necro-police,
who can outrun the grave-y train?
Along with Longfellow I regard the bomb-
gods of this world and see that there
is no peace on earth, no lasting good-will
between men, and hate mocks the carols.

Oh, Cool Christmas, prove me wrong!
Christmas, my Wenceslas, save us!

Who Does Death Belong To?

In the wake of witnessing
the fraternal guillotine, Victor
Hugo's Bienvenu queried,
"By what right do men
touch that unknown thing?"
The Bishop gave Death
to God, but does God
own Jack the Grim Reaper,
or is this 100-percent killer a
freelancer cast from the vacant
belly of *tsimtsum*, The Emptiness?

Who made the guillotine?
The judge and the carpenter.
Who deals out death best?
The humanitarian.

Hugo described the guillotine
as a willful, carnivorous creature,
a non-neutral executioner's partner
— and replacing "guillotine" with
"the Bomb" still makes perfect sense.
In fact, Victor Hugo predicted the Nuke.

There Is No Dignity in Death

Corpses are the stupidest things on Earth,
guileless clowns, not revered skulls of Yoricks.

One eye wide open and one half-closed.
Is that a smile or a frown?

Grandfather, Grandfather!
I can't get your corpse out of my mind.

Who wants to be near these nobodies?
Nobody.

They make me feel more alone than alone.
They're always ahead in time; I'm an infant.

They've escaped wars, harsh winters, heartache.
The dead don't fret over death and taxes.

I can't forget your once-strong arms, hands.
Alas, Grandfather, I knew you once.
I don't want to stare like you, gape like you.

One eye wide open and one half-closed: Penthouse
centerfolds, Tutsis, Queen Victoria, MLK, James Dean.

My soul chills at Bruegel the Elder's *The Triumph of Death*
and Holbein the Younger's *Dead Christ in the Tomb*!

Are you enjoying the buffet, triumphant worms?
Festive erasers, maybe your gluttony is mercy.

What is death's most fearsome statement? "It is over."
I mourn, I weep for everyone — everyone — who has died before.

Dead man, tell me tales.
Let me know if there is Hereafter.

Lilies of the field and birds of the air have no fear,
but I am neither lily nor bird.

I dread death, no matter the consolation or leaks
of faith, despite respite from Pascal's doubtful shivers.
Only death is grown on the Body Farm.

Grandfather, Grandfather!

Titan Arum/Corpse Flower

The Titan Arum or "corpse flower":
a dwindling and rarely blooming
mystery resembling a ghoulish phallus
spearing up from an impressive spathe.
This tropical wonder mocks our mortality
and heckles with its reek, since it attracts
carnivorous insects by producing sulfur,
cadaverine and putrescine (key chemicals
in decomposition's process) and stinks like
a rotting human body. Though we may
admire the plant's odd majesty, our whiffs
transmit a conscious or subconscious reminder
of our eventual decay. As if this isn't enough,
after fertilization the Titan blooms with red-orange
fruits which resemble beach-bimbo breasts and
contrast hags' or female corpses' raisined dugs.
After a life of three days, the Titan's flower dies,
but a 20-foot quasi-tree springs up in its place.
Eventually, this magnificent thing starts the cycle
of Titan life all over again — while our physical destiny
is to exhale one last time, wilt and dissolve, molder,
then vitamin flowers.

Spiritual Giants

Anatomy = destiny?

In 1974 five-foot-six funambulist Philippe Petit, a man
with a relatively small build (to match his surname), rose
from the obscure streets and dueled the void between
New York City's Twin Towers on a tightrope, and 27 years later whoever
bastardminded 9/11/2001 turned the stately edifices *into*
a void, felled them to the level of the obscure streets.

David, Goliath.
Samurai, Mao Tse-tung.
Bethlehem manger, Oval Office.
Kitty Hawk, Kremlin.
Prada, *Pravda*.

Tubman, Legree, Hobbit, Sauron.
The difference between MLK's
"I have a dream" and Stalin's
"Death solves all problems."

I'm So over the Rainbow

1)

The French's *Opération Satanique* sank
Greenpeace's *Rainbow Warrior* because
it threatened a Moruroan nuke test.

The U.S.'s Operation Restore Hope in
Somalia ended in carnage and naked
Ranger corpses dragged, ripped and
beaten by savages.

2)

Paul Tibbets, pilot of Enola Gay (his mommy's
name) and dropper of the Bomb on Hiroshima,
reenacted his crime at a Texas air show in 1976.

There's not an ounce of apology in him
because, as he told The Gray Lady, his
mission was "one to save lives."

"Sorry is only a five-lettered word," Manson-girl
Leslie Van Houten said.

3)

Jacobin Saint-Just, who had a fiery brain
and an icy heart, was promoted to board
member of the Committee of Public Safety
during the fraternal Reign of Terror.

4)

The name of India's first tested nuke in 1974?
"The Smiling Buddha."

5)

Serial killer, corpse-collector and cannibal
Jeffrey Dahmer lobotomized victims in his
*

quest for forever-loyal male lovers. He did
it for love, for love, he did it for love, for love.

6)

Peace, warrior, peace.

Leap to Conquer

As I step into and out of the shower, I cringe at the betrayal
of our jelly-filled integument: exposed flesh's incision-begging,
how it repels water and sips air but welcomes the torturer's
blade, hook, scalpel as favored invaders freeing unseen seams.

We are thin bubbles in our translucent birthday suits.

What could be more glorious and pitiful than a naked human?
There are universes between Debbie Harry and Ono/Lennon.
A perfect-10 earth angel panting in ecstasy one minute: a bald
ape when barred from bathing, a horrid slab when dead.

To survive, you have to build yourself upward like a cathedral,
shield the scrotum (that pitiful pudendal pendulum) or the vulva,
dress in layers and layers and layers as if tundra-whipped: be an
enigma-wrapped riddle, a firewalled room, buried jewels.

The costume, the uniform, designer duds are our fortresses, for
genocide is usually a big peep show: a blur of pubic triangles,
depressed breasts, frozen toes, gaping thighs, shriveled buttocks.
Corpse piles mock sex orgies: faces muffled by rotten genitals.

"We are fearfully and wonderfully made," as the Psalm goes.
Does the mirror, do morgues and battlefields, lie?
Psalm, overwhelm me.
Tell me the truth.

Be Like Water

I've never met a fire that has started itself, the lazy things.
Fire's a child of ignition.
Yes, we did start the fire, people.

It's a tongue shot from human tongues, scorching invective,
hell's music, hate's and fear's hands.
George Washington said it's like ineloquent government.

I hardly blink when earth sets herself on fire, opens up to
roar and takes our Lego homes with her into perdition.
Natural disasters bore me to tearlessness, are dull givens.

But when humans ignite atrocity, my heart screams:
*Be like water, body around me — otherwise I burn like paper,
burn like lint, burn quickly if kissed by fire!*

(If there's no God, God help us.)

The Ever-Grinning Skull

I've been told that the river flows despite our sinks and swims,
that boughs break and cradles fall, that we can't stop the wind
when it vipers tornadic or the embittered ocean stampedes
humaned land — but these are dumb and natural things, mindless,
blameless events that belong to the same unaware family as
erosion and decay: scorpions sting, mongooses eggjack turtle
spawn, wolves massacre, earth belches and swallows freeways
and rush-hour crowds, pretty plants poison, pretty berries kill.

Then what is to blame in the human heart?
Aren't passions scorpions?
Aren't hates and envies wolves?
Aren't genitals upset tectonics, riots poisons,
diseased gigolos and whores deadly fruits?
Can stuff from stuff be enough to justify "whatever,"
or are we held to a different standard than oceans
and wind, not absolved by a plea of "the double
helix made me do it," ripe for reprimand when our
hands are caught in cookie jars, when we let murder
leap from us like a sudden and deafening song?

You say there's good and evil in the heart of man, that there's
a choice involved in the rotation of this inner globe that is central
to the vicious circus of personality. You say that, though this unique
muscle is set into and kept in motion by purely physical forces, we
can slow or halt the spin according to self-evident moral vibes —
and those who break urge-checking rules deserve correction by
mass opinion, righteous coercion, the legal gavel's knock or "tsk-tsk."

Do me a favor and close your scriptures, fold your pamphlets,
turn off *Mister Rogers*, mute your "kumbaya, my Lord" and face me
face to face, bare wire to bare wire: confess that you've faced
the Abyss and saw nothing look back, that when you called into
it you heard no echo or reply — only sound vanishing into airless
space, that your prayers seem to die in mid-air, that you feel
the presence of absence in "intimate" exchanges.

Behold a lover's or spouse's smile. Further in: buccinators!
Orbicularis oris! Maxilla, mandible, mastoid, muscles' ugly strati,
veiny veins, sinewy sinews, bones down to osteon.

Behind every winning smile or frown is a constant skull grin.
Painter Schiele shows us skeletons under lying woman skin.
"Don't run," I whisper to the quaking rabbit. "I won't hurt you,
darling creature." Then I imagine gnashing into its raw throat
in inevitable someday-starvation's mad and pity-blind delirium.
Where is the love in all of this, unseen Sire?
Where are "I Am" and "Thou Art" in this Abyss?
Do all roads lead to graves, to worms' dinners?
Good King Wenceslas, I've lost my footing in the storm!
Explode my fear and despair with your warm poetry!

Do me a favor and open your scriptures, unfold your pamphlets,
turn on *Mister Rogers*, hum your "kumbaya, my Lord" and face me
face to face, bare wire to bare wire: watching each other like holes
attempting penetration until (like after chanting "Bloody Mary" into
mirrors) something appears, something happens, something goes
down, something sparks in the abysmal dark: our faces from before
we were born appear as cores of water ripples or deltas of lightcones.

Sartre said that man's inhumanity to man springs from scarcity, but, no,
it springs from abundance! From plenitude! From bloat and boredom!
We're imprisoned by *utter* freedom, sentenced to a total lack of barrier
and to be free to do whatever is imaginable: as quickly as bricks to heads
can turn scholars into vegetables, I could gnash your lips away without
warning, you could rake my eyeballs to shreds with clawed hands.

Any horror — *any* horror — you can muster in that two-thousand/two-
thousand-vision eye (the imagination) has happened, is happening,
will happen at one time or another, and behind every atrocity is a face
shaming the pre-birth face whose mouth is turned down at sin and waste,
its fetal soul appalled at what it sees when summoned to our adult mirror-
faces: our hearts of darkness. (If there's no God, God help us.)

Tread my footprints, my good poet,
don't fret when you walk in them.
Though freedom allows blood to flow,
know it sharpens your pen,
know it is the heart's psalm,
know eternity happens soon.

Black Dahlia Nihilismus

> *Dreadful symmetry: The Black Dahlia's real name*
> *was Liz Short. The nickname of Elizabeth Stride, one*
> *of Jack the Ripper's victims, was Long Liz.*

Elizabeth Short:
tortured, sundered
in half at the torso,
right nipple torn
off, face like forked
steak, knife carved
a smile like the Joker's,
your parts arranged
with a devil's care.

Beth, Betty, Black Dahlia:
waitress waiting to be an
actress, loner melancholia
on Hollywood Boulevard,
blue eyes and raven-hair.

Pummeled, bruised, stabbed,
drained of blood, force-fed
feces, desecrated, legs spread
(foresty pudenda), dumped in a lot.
Did your killer fear *vagina dentata*
or impotence at your virgin threshold?
I spit at you, Hollywood!

Black Dahlia found dead January 15, 1947.
Bleak David born January 16, 1973.
Marie Antoinette beheaded October 16, 1793.
Add one to Dahlia's January and one to my year,
reverse her 47 and subtract one from it.
Switch the 7 and 9 in the Queen's death year,
keep the day and rewind nine months.

This is synchropsychosympathy.

I Am Your Beloved Liar, Dear Daughter, Dear Son

The transgressed hymen and
first wet dream are not the worst
loss of innocence. The worst is
anticipation of the lonely fact
of death, the lifetime guarantee
that it will come sooner or later.

Oh, the look in your eyes,
my children, when you find the
bones beyond the dreamy
crib, learn the open secret
that there's a morning when
your dear eyes will not open.

For now, live in the shadow of my
loving lie, this lifesaving fib left
to each new generation, this
merciful suffocation of vacuum,
lightlessness and lightlessnessless,
the coffin, that final bedroom.

It's the cruelest abuse that will
bruise you, God's biggest sin.
If I could massacre every corpse
and raid the kingdom of worms
myself, I would, dearest children,
dearest ones, you who will die.

Kyrie Logos and EverMySon

For my children

I stand corrected, daughter, son.
My despair is the lie, my fear is
the cruelest abuse, my anger
at God my biggest sin.

I am an insult, a buffoon,
an easy-path taker: lorn
and turned on by being lorn,
a Psalmic Eeyore with a lost tail.

Theses butt theses, and moods
muddy the never-still waters.
One minute there is a future,
in the next all is passed and past.

Yes, vanity and palaces, charity
and churches all become dust,
but what Gompertz calls "sparks
of spirit" ignite it as gunpowder.

Hypocrite me, if I believe
that we are all captives
of the Reaper, why live
as if life is the wiser choice?
There's a gaping skull
at the door — but it has
no power to enter, dears.
It's powerless, darlings.

You, daughter and son, are the correction.
You are the most difficult path I've taken:
one leading to trust in life.

I'm a sire sired by the Sire of sires.

Your conceptions debunked my woes,
shattered my belief in death, pinned
a ribbon on this Pslamic Eeyore's tail.

Save Me, Coffin

> *Up from the spray of thy ocean-perishing —*
> *straight up, leaps thy apotheosis!*
> — *Ishmael*, Moby-Dick

Believing himself to be imperiled
by cannibal harpooner Queequeg
(his near-future friend), in Peter Coffin's
Spouter-Inn, Melville's Ishmael cried
foreshadowingly: "Coffin! Angels! Save me!"

Believing himself to be dying on
the Ahab-run, tooth-studded *Pequod*,
Queequeg requested a coffin-canoe
be built so that he could float past
celestial archipelagoes, but he chose
life, and the coffin was made into a life-buoy.

Believing himself unmanned of Man,
death-free on sea and land, keener
than the quadrant he trampled with
foot and bone peg (rightly cursing
"vain toy" science), Ahab heard
the Parsee's occult promise "that
neither hearse nor coffin can be thine."

Believing himself to be doomed
by a whirlpool, after Ahab stung
the Great Whale and bade death
to "sink all coffins and all hearses
to one common pool," Ish testified
that he was saved by the life-buoy
coffin, an odd angel shot from the depths.

Lucid Delirium 2

This wretched illness is a fountain.
A pure one, aside from
the filth gush.

A fountain, cleansing. Killing incidentals,
trivia. Drowning hecklers,
parasites.

What do I hear in its waters?
That I'm the only awake man.
What do I see in its waters?
That I'm gnarled by sin and in
need of redemption, that I mustn't
forget when I'm well again.

Fearful, don't fear!
Dying, don't despair!
Sleepers, awake!

Destroy distractions!
Flush all medications!
Unplug the power grids!
Cancel all classes, seminars, sermons!
Trash the marketplaces, manumit Man!

Thank you, crushing illness,
for this death of dignity,
for clearing mirrors.

I vomited myself from myself, cast from
Leviathan's bowels, and found
myself on a mountain.

Fearful, don't fear!
Dying, don't despair!
Sleepers, awake!

Wretched illness, you recalibrate me.
I see that there's a Shadow of Light behind.

Come to the mountain.

Straw Dog (The Cool Comes)

Despite this endless wall of horror,
I must knock until I find the Door.
Like Aldous Huxley's Savage arguing
poetry and God against *Brave New
World*'s Shakespeare-/Bible-banning
Controller, or like Captain Ahab
monologuing against pulverizing Fate,
I advocate Personality over Anonymity,
cling to the whispering Shadow as torrents
of bright blindness try to wash Me away.

*Straighten the swastika,
hammer the sterile sickle
(that futile question mark)
into a fertile exclamation point!*

Shadow of Light, you know my private
dirges: you are the cantilever that holds
me safely over Apocalypse, you are
the Frank Lloyd Wright of my spiritual
estate, a Philippe Petit guiding me from
tower to tower, the Shadow-caster
in agon with Gomorrah's false sun.

*This Psalmic Eeyore has a
restored tail, wears a ribbon
to show his marriage to both
Half-Empty and Half-Full.*

Though I walk through death's valley,
scale mountains of skulls, capsize on
mystery-seas, I shall not crave *schema*
or all-revealing and blinding Reason.

The Cool comes: the wintry summer, the sub-zero fire.
My half-empty cup runs over with Keats' Negative Capability:
juggling contradictions without forcing wholeness,
without stuffing the world into a proper box.

Where Are You, Who You Are?

for T.S. Eliot

Who You Are, I don't want to live as if dead.
I want to shun eaves during rain, unafraid of a soaking.
My feet are bleeding, my bones are splintered.
My finest hours have been stupored minutes.

I give up this Apocalypse I've been hoarding!
I've been dreaming from a grave, mistaking the
constant siege for the imperiled but pure citadel.

My grief soaks the heavens like upward rain,
my heart holds an insurmountable mountain.
I'm why-curious, incapable of indifference.

This corpse wants to live, so hold down your hand,
Who You Are, take my reaching-since-the-womb hand.
Save me from the devil's businessmen, revolutionaries'
killing floors, fetus-snuffers and daughter-soilers.

I've been so careful drawing the map that I've covered
no ground, become agoraphobized, vestigialed
my legs, taken root in a sterile, ugly wasteland.
I pluck this hair shirt, kick off these shackles!

Run from Kafka to Capra,
set fire to Hades' flames,
disdain determinism, run
to Capra, my son, my son.
My hand reached out for yours
before yours reached out for mine.

Dada. Die, David. De-lovely.
Shekinah shekinah shekinah

SERMON

Beautylicious

For John Ruskin and James Whistler

Is art opiate or catalyst, moral or amoral, bauble or end-all?
I'm pendulous between Whistler and Ruskin, cheering
art autonomism, then plumbing goddesses for godliness.
People, aesthetics is the milk of humankindness.

What lofty correspondence can be found in overrated,
homely *Mona Lisa*? Give me and cartoonist R. Crumb a
bootylicious, robust Boucher or Manet bather, or an Art Deco
De Lempicka debutante, not a Lotto or man-wild Michelangelo.

Should looks or Logos be the blood of the visual-art canon?
Does Walter Pater's "art for art's sake" trump moral evaluation?

Since man-free Nature is barren, as Blake says, Beauty's
humanity's vanity, which projects, doesn't receive, standards.
Unheard falling trees don't make sound, nor are sunsets on
rivertops or snowdrifts gorgeous without the human gaze.

Though aurorae engross and lion prides impress,
such givens are hairs'-breadths away from frostbite
and picked-clean human ribcages. (You say we're
only Nature too? Mascara and perfume refute.)

The world is our imaginations' canvas, said Thoreau.
The Sublime in us vibrates with the Sublime without.

Brevity is Beauty's soul, this uncertain something that
glows in certain someones for seemingly forever until it
vanishes (doesn't fade), is gone as suddenly as virginity,
which, like Beauty, leaves a loud wake in its absence.

Blake found "the head Sublime" and "the genitals Beauty,"
and critic Gautier saw our basic response to Beauty as erotic,
not holy or indicative of eternal Platonic Forms, but tied directly
to the hot and sexy externals: Ingres' Grande Odalisque's toes.

Beauty is immediate, is, is itself, gestalt —
but when moralized: mastectomized!

Then again, Ayn Rand rightfully scorned the "esthetic vacuum"
of the twentieth century (which is a heck of a lot worse in this
twenty-first). Art is a moral manifestation, a conceptual gauge:
it recreates reality according to values, so ugly art is anti-Man.

She insisted that art is an "ought," not an "it is," not a "because I
felt like it," not a canvas on which to display misshapen miseries
but a Romantic expression of objective volition, harmony.
Amen, Rand! Cold sores have no place on beautiful lips!

Imperfections, however, liberate expression, says Ruskin: they
make things lovelier, and only those who misunderstand art
demand perfection from it: the accurate gauge of a nation's
ultimate ruin is its drive to attain perfect artistic power.

*Shun Naturalists for their embracement of blemish and blight, but
trust Ruskin's distrust of an aesthetic that's too right and too "on."*

When Irving Howe praised Ellison's "Negro novel," *Invisible Man*, Ellison
insisted that it transcended race and sociopolitical programs, and turned
black suffering into universal art, just as blues music rises above its painful
inspiration: because art is its own importance, its own social action.

Art may be mimetic in intention, said Auden, but it's not life,
it's *fait accompli*, not society's midwife — who would want it
to lock steps with in-vogue vulgarity and political fads, earn
gold stars for correctness, glorify warts, the Fact, the Statistic?

Delacroix (enthraller of Baudelaire) insisted that Nature is
a dictionary that some artists reference and others transcribe,
and Oscar Wilde's Vivian warned of Nature's destruction of Art —
how lying decays while we sell ourselves "for a mess of facts."

*Stand with Helmut Newton against dismal Diane Arbus!
To* not *doctor what's seen is to make sick. Lie to us!*

Sight alone is painting's purview, according to Magritte.
Only mediocrities cater to other things over spectators' eyes.
Genius paintings don't express ideas or emotions but only
mysterious images that sensationalize the familiar day-to-day.

Such paintings disallow meditation, jolting spectators awake
to dream-like realization for only a moment that defies capture
and leaves them dissatisfied with lackluster "reality": forever
inclining them to skies made of wood and eyes made of skies.

A glass of water atop an open umbrella and a face made
of a woman's torso aren't Hegelian or feminist commentary.

Why do women-shamers cover all but females' eyes while
they really crave to crawl their bodies like Escher reptiles
on endless stairs, caught in a lustful loop, a bitter charade,
forever distracted from prayers and ablution?

Picasso must've hated the female nude (why else the abuse?),
and Rouault saw prostitutes as grim whales rather than as sootier
cousins of odalisques so etherealized by Manet, Ingres and Matisse.
He who curses such women has a bone to pick with himself.

In "The Lure of Beauty" H.L. Mencken called the female form
defective, like "a drunken dollar-mark" from the side.

Though Delvaux knew the skeleton within the nude earth-angel,
he celebrated (along with Courbet) the knowing bush instead
of vapid baldness, the shadowy thicket rather than the sunny
patio — unlike this era's fixation with the mown infantile gash.

No one model sufficed while Raphael composed the *Galatea*,
so he compiled parts of multiple models and other depictions,
Poliziano's poetry, others' art — not from nature itself, not from
a factual given, but from a Frankenstinian ideal.

Kenneth Clarke saw flashes of universal order in our bodies,
and Blake saw women's nakedness as God's work.
Coco Chanel: well-dressedness is next to nakedness.
Rousseau: "We are not our clothes." Baudelaire: Oh, we *are*!

Ditto, Baudelaire. Nature's a monster factory and Woman
(in whom "there is everything," said Chanel) transcends the
disgusting Real. Adornment earns her adoration and idolaters'
praise; dress and decoration plus born-body sparks supernature.

Woman is a reflecting pool, an unnavigable forest, deep and
black and impure: unhumble Garbo-Bardot pin-up geisha!

Just as wise Ruskin saw that all life is both decaying and becoming,
Baudelaire double-thought about temporal angels: praising their
powerful charms while anticipating the stench of their future corpses.
However, they live whole and fragrant in survivors' minds'-eyes.

Beautiful minx, a strategic bunker-grave, layered and layered,
proofed and proofed, can keep the worms from breaching the
flesh that sings cataract-counteracting songs into men's jaded
sight, but self-digestion and catabolism are enemies within, dear.

*"The tomb always understands the poet," Baudelaire wrote.
Both know both sides of the final door of the courtesan's exit.*

Art for art's sake bugged Kandinsky, who believed art is progressive
expression of the Eternal, color exercises spirit, an "inner need" births
Beauty, and artists, as Beauty's priests, must guide others to the spirit-
pyramid's pinnacle: ever forward, ever rising, potent but inert.

If artists shirk the duty of guidance and evolution, they and their
spectators become alienated, and works become baubles, not
end-alls, souls go adrift, the glove loses the hand: but Kandy had
no theoretical process — only total abstraction and ultra-subjectivity.

Francis Schaeffer rebuts that abstraction *is* the alienating culprit,
for incoherent art cannot contain moral inspiration or achieve
speech: anti-Renaissance Picasso fragmented the world and man
(except, curiously, in key portraits of his beloved wives and children).

*Can the eternal be expressed through squiggles and geometrics,
readymades, drips and splats and color-diarrheal Pollocks?*

What would Nietzsche say of Picasso, Duchamp, Klee, Francis Bacon?
Would it terrify his eye to "find man broken up, and scattered about,
as on a battle- and butcher-ground," or would he chalk up their work
to Dionysian dissolution, a trough in the Will wave, a wink at Chaos?

For Nietzsche art's eternal essence lies in the genius and the primal
architect melding in amoral acts of creation and destruction, divinity
regarding itself through its works' eyes: beauty shining in form and
sublimity revealed in revelrous disfigurement and form-devoidance.

*He and Kandinsky shared belief in spiritual synesthesia: musical
colors for Kandy and mythical music for Freddy, uplifting for both.*

Does the universe flow from original Beauty, as Emerson claims,
and is that why even a child detects distortions in pictures and
hearts kick at first sight of a pleasant form? Don't bother touring
in search of beauty unless it's packed in your bags, Emerson warns.

Whatever its nature or supernature, art and Beauty are melancholy:
we can't separate them from That Empty Feeling, from shortfallenness.
Painter Hopper hated flowers for their self-contained beauty, their
impermeability and opaqueness to our selves.

Part 4:
The Pink Cathedral

[Y]et even in its smallest sections the human body kept its beauty.
— Doctor Zhivago

Nature . . . combines the organ of its highest fulfillment, the organ of generation, with the organ of urination . . . Speech and kissing, on the one hand, and eating, drinking and spitting on the other, are all done with the mouth.
— Hegel, *The Phenomenology of Spirit*

Outspoken buttocks in pink beads . . . The world's one flagrant, sweating cinch.
— Hart Crane, *The Bridge*

Is the Spirit a Bone?

You think that you can think apart from your parts?
Sojourn purely mentally or spiritually?
Astrally project away from that decaying clay?

Don't you know that the spirit is a bone?
That $E = mc^2$ was marrow as much as mentation?

You think you can't think?
That there's nirvana, that there's time-out?
That we can cut the umbilical cord and rise?

Spontaneity

Spontaneous lovemaking
is a roulette because who
knows when the sexy dew
becomes eggy soup in the
hours between soap and
soap, or if bacteria has
lacquered the teeth and
sheathed the ever-humid
tongue like sausage casing?

It's like fleeing around an un-
known corner and tumbling
down a hill: shocked at
the irreversibility, a counter-
clockwise swirl, not being able
to rebottle the genie: the upward
coital momentum stopped by
a sudden plummet from the
Galatean pedestal.

Morning Breath

Mornings after in movies don't move me because they're
based on a greasy premise: that our mouths are sweetmeats
after salty all-night bacterial orgies, that our crannies stave
off stench many hours after cleansing.

Mouths of hotties are no more immune than hags' maws,
Venusian visages sag like sunken *Titanic*s, mascara runs away,
perfume evaporates and dinners inflate bowel balloons.

Eyes are obsessive Photoshoppers, but nostrils narrow at
subpar odors, vision being lust's cockpit and the snobbish nose
being the organ of the strongest attraction or revulsion.

The Matrix

When thighs exhale jungle centuries
prehistory brays, kicks.

The Charleston is a dolled-up Ashanti funerary dance.
Dark dada atavismus haunts the discotheques.

Boom, boom: the drums, the drums in us.
Who knew this best but the Victorians?

Faceslick
Unlocked odor
Noxiouslicious
Super-californiagirl-lust-sexreek-suffocatious.

Caress to Teeth

Once they taste it, they crave it.
Once skirts lift they never lower.
The body is an undousable wildfire.

My Little Pony turns to "Saddle, spur me."
Barbie pleads, "Crush, chew, own me."
Shirley Temple has a Deep Throat,
Lolita emerges from the sweaty Haze,
Minerva bows to Pallas.

The Land of Oz and Wonderland are
virginity lost. You can't go back home.
"Off with her [maiden]head!"

What is this sea-change from caress to teeth?
Where is the love-born soul?
What is this whore in us?

The Roaring Woman

I want to suck her legs.

Could chew through titanium to gain entrance.
Would wallow in any fluid, any filthiness, any caught illness.
There's no argument against her ecstatic gibberish,
no syllogism in the face of her hate-kisses,
no hope for affection in this writhing murderess.

Where have my Goody Two-Shoes and clean upbringing gone?
Were all those spankings and punitive deprivations in vain?

Her legs howl.
Her Lucifernal jungle.
Her rapist locks.

What species is this predator-animal with such hammering hips?
Who can outrun this undulant-rumped *clickclack*ing high-heeled hell angel?
Those knees are shrunken skulls, those ankles are candied cyanide,
those toes are fatal berries, those foot bones are belladonna roots.

Unlady, your thighs steam forth an event horizon.
My death begs to be born between them.

The Devil Is an Ass

I love/hate the living, fluxing flesh, the ever-dying flesh.
Venus is a cannibal flytrap, skin is leviathan-filled brine.

It's why pornography is such a paradoxical intoxicant:
nakedness' implied violence, tooth as nail and tongue as cudgel.

But its vulnerability also is a whispered promise: "Trust me
and I'll trust you," openness opens for openness.

We are smut's marionettes at first sight, the saliva strings pull us in.
Sodom's real estate is priceless for a reason.

Genital dilation and hole-gapes, the rampant scrub of pubic hair,
the glutton grunts, the gasping gasps, the rule of dumb limbs.

Scientists, lawyers, heads of state, social workers, nurses: splatter into
a mess of saliva, flapping buttocks, sweat and breath, "More!"

There's an eelish beauty in the Rorschach blot of wringing bodies,
between Manichaean mortification and Larry Flynt.

Wonder, however: is there God in this? Where is the love?
Does every DNA contain an "I am," a "Thou art"?

Every "she"/"he" is "it" in both porn and post-mortem.
"We" cease to be "me" and "you," become most improper nouns.

Porn's bizarre exuberance flouts the triumph of grave worms,
the lifeful squish and smells effigize death's pus and gas.

(What strange bedfellows we befriend in our love-ins against the Reaper.)

There's horror in savage pleasure and glee in distressed flesh: the Shoah,
1994 Rwanda, Ed Gein, Black Dahlia, grunting porn-star Sasha Grey.

Queen Barbie

To get rid of Barbie you'd have to drive a
silver stake through her plastic heart.
— Anna Quindlen

Tomboy Ruth Handler
didn't dig dolls as a child
but when she became
a Mattel co-founder,
learned toys' power
(thanks to her husband's
toymaking genius) and
saw that paper dolls
hampered the inter-
changeability of fashion,
she designed Barbie,
a miniature mannequin
with breasts(!) and
haute couture.

Female-chauvinists
savage the craze,
claiming that it causes
poor body image
among girls who fall
short of Barbie's dimensions,
as if she began a pandemic
of dysmorphophobia,
set the bar so high
that each girl owner
sees herself as a hopeless
Dolly Dimples.

(Ask conscription-eligible
males if "Be all you can
be" is better than "Be who
you wanna be.")

Anna Quindlen hates Barbie
and thinks she should die
as every vampire should:
with "a silver stake through
her plastic heart," not realizing
that it's the clothes,
not the body, stupid —
and maybe pissed
that the doll lacks a
monologuing vagina.

After a mastectomy
due to breast cancer,
Ruth started another
company, Ruthton,
which specialized in
bra prostheses for
fellow depressed
patients, ironically
boosting female body
image with faux parts.

Victoria's Secret Angels

Their belly buttons:
inward puckers,
evidence of descendance,
(once womb-wired)
cloistered ex-orifices.
Umbilici-leidoscope.

Careful, gazer, careful.
There's no answer there.
What you crave is far-off.
Hot bodies are roadside Sirens.

My mind's eyes are lost
like Hansel and Gretel
in a candybody.

Living milk,
living fire,
living-living.

Lawful Carnal Knowledge

Altruistic law states that the gorgeous lose
looks the worse they behave and the so-so
cuten when their "inner beauty" surfaces and shines.

This second premise has paved loveways for homelies
and uglies like Lyle Lovett, Margaret Fuller, Emma Goldman,
Stephen Hawking, but the first premise is a feel-good fib.

Because natural law gives esteem to handsome
villains and movie-perfect gun molls, hands down.
Despite deceit, crime, loutishness and lunacy, sexy
humans malleate principled minds, obliterate righteous
offense, burn sermons, erase manifestos.

You may not ever admit it or even feel it, but there
is a pure nymphomaniac stowed away in a box in a box
in a crate in a crate in a hold in a hold deep inside you.
All it does is want and crave, worship flesh for flesh's sake.

The average and homely are masochized by and indenture
themselves to Adonis and Aphrodite: "We live to serve you in
storm and stress, at our expense, until we wither and pass while
your visages and bodies live on, grand studs, fair ladies."

Unless personality and sexuality mesh, one either
makes love to outer or so-called inner beauty in this
arena of hungry one-night stands and "butterfaces."

Crushing on Eva Braun

What happens to a fashionista deferred?

Does she shrivel under the Fatherland's shadow?
Or snap photos and roll reels of the Nazi inner circle
while wishing that some proto-Paparazzo, armed
to the teeth with cameras, would storm the Berghof
like Robin Hood and tatter her cloister's privacy?

Does she feel like a joyless clown in her dirndl dress
when she could be sporting Hugo Boss or relishing
the bourgeois cosmetics of Aphroditism during
the Fuhrer's and Bormann's absence?

Eva, they tend to remember you as Hitler mistress
and eleventh-hour wife, as failed photographer
dressed and mugging in Jolsonian blackface, as
dutiful thrall dispatched by a cyanide breath mint.

But I gawk at your Grable-grade legs and guiltily
view your underrated grace in leftover home movies:
you and Blondi, you skiing, you on ice skates, you
so darling in a bathing suit (your wave-foamy feet),
your hair's bounce — such a smile, such a nose, a face.

Eva Braun, what you could have been.

Fallen from the blue heights of the Obersalzberg
to the Plutonian bowels of the Berlin bunker,
your ashes are burned again and again by
history's juries, but I'll whisper a truth in my heart:

I'm a little in love with you, Eva Anna, fashionista
deferred, and I both understand and resent that
you chose not to sag under the heavy load of age
and guilt, that you followed through with ignominy.

Burn softly, foolish devil-mate.
Unborn diva — explode!

Vanity

Where would my nose for Beauty lead me,
to what lengths would vanity drive me in
search for the fairest fair, Perfect Tens, Eights, Fives?

If time rejackbooted the fall of Weimar and
the disease-blossom of National Socialism,
would my disgust for Dix and Brecht bedevil me?

Beware the lure of *Glaube and Schonheit* (Beauty and Faith).

My hygienic fixations, my Swiftian fear of shit,
the hypnosis of bathed bodies and scents:
would these build a ghetto wall, a snobbery,
echo Zimbardo's Stanford prison experiment?

Can lust for Nordic living dolls lock steps with Klaus Barbie?

A Jewish skeleton-woman with infected skin,
hairy-faced from ceased menses, drags herself to me.
My nostrils fill with her stink, my body cringes as
if every centimeter of separation helps prevent
contagion or indelible odor . . .

Despite its *kitsch* and banal fixation, wasn't Nazi art
appreciation a soft spot for the angels of our nature,
the Sublime beyond the mass Asshole they forged?

Should I shiver at Hitler's and my taste for nudes, Rubens, Boucher?

. . . She reveals a rickety hand from the sewer dark
of her rancid shawl and struggles to extend a finger,
reminding me of 2001: A Space Odyssey*'s super-aged*
Dave Bowman pointing at the silent monolith from his
deathbed, pointing with mute understanding . . .

A nose for Beauty and fair things drove art-looter Goering to
stock a Xanadu of plundered pulchritude, hold Leonardo's
Lady With an Ermine (she of painting history's loveliest hands)
hostage, cram the cream of the art crop into Salzburg's salt mines,
even buy forger Van Meergeren's fake Vermeer and play the dupe.

Does my gadfly-chase of the Gibson Girl make me a dupe as well?
Do I pedestal Galatea at the expense of despised Elephant Men,
in blindness to the ugly horrors performed in the name of aesthetic
order, eye-friendly symbology and symmetrical ideals?

. . . To her I must seem a corpulent god, a fragrant giant
who has the power — the right — to grind her under my
boot, to stomp her stink into the dirt that is her superior
sister, that even her past self (now a teasing dream)
was fit only to serve as bridge over cesspuddles . . .

My God, what have I done?
My fetishes have become atrocious.
Hardcore highs have soured me against subtle stimulants.

If a half-dead, diseased Jewish woman slithered
through the ghetto wall and begged me for help,
would my fear of bodily breakdown benumb me?
Has the physical ideal led me into Fuhrers' chambers?
Have I filled boxcars with negatives of my photographic eye?

No. No!
Piss on the Aryan ideal!
Mercy hath not eyes, not nostrils.

The Nose of the World

1)

What's in a nose?
Noses get in their owners' way
or nudge them toward untoward
ends — and worse means.

Try to minimize a large nose with
cosmetic tricks or hire a surgeon
to reshape or subtract from it,
but there's no permanent escape.

2)

Andy Warhol's refused reform,
forcing him to draw eyes else-
where with strawy wigs and those
shameful, shameful glasses.

3)

Will world-harried Jews ever outrun
pestilential physiognomy that says
a Jew nose is a nose is a nose as
verminous as Leonardo's Judas?
(I holler "J'accuse" with Zola eternally!)

And who can gloss over Adolf Hitler's
schnoz, which grew to bulldog pro-
portions from his little corporal days
to the bunker: proof of doubles?

4)

That downward slide of Stalin's proboscis
sceptored over state-sponsored famines,
rhinoplasty turned *Dirty Dancing*'s
Jennifer Grey fame-proof.

5)

Anais Nin, that bottomless slut, had
her nose redone but she poked it into
sexual excess upon excess, careless
abortions, immeasurable despair.

She fled monotony and cackled from
bed to bed — including her own father's:
like-nose to like-nose sniffing in genetic
familiars, living the Freudian dream.

Until that chick's end came home to roost
and her vagina got cancer, taming that
rabid Nin libido and damning her to a
loverless, self-stale sickbed, deathbed.

6)

Among the Wild West's Tombstone's
"Shady Ladies" was "Big Nose" Kate
Elder, wife of and stool pigeon against
a name everyone knows: Doc Holliday.

7)

Saint-Just looked down his nose at the
Ancien Regime and sniffed the Terror's
stench with relish for "Liberty is a bitch who
must be bedded on a mattress of corpses."

8)

Rule exception: Cyrano de Bergerac schooled
the Viscount on how to properly whip slick
quips against his profound proboscis, like
reversing slurs and epithets by humorizing them.
When he (via Ed Rostand) extemporized a

ballade as a witty follow-up (seventy years
before Kool Herc, The Last Poets and Bronx
jams) ten-hearted Cyrano created hip hop!

Dying fifteen years after his Arras wound, Love's
humble Pinocchio told Roxanne that he penned
those "love-words" all that time before swiping his
sword at Death and dying clutching his *panache*.

9)

Aside: Dali's *Face of Mae West* features sofa
"lips" and a fireplace "nose." West was born
the same year as "Schnozzola" Jimmy Durante.

10)

Myrna Loy's nose.

Bouguereau Girl

Let down your air, pure one, for the vacuum is filling me.

There is no purity but you are pure, there is no air but you have air,
there is no sanctuary but you are a safe church.

Masses would worship your strawberry, waste-free
Venusvaporous ass, Picasso would be compelled
to paint you straight, you'd divide war divisions if
you strode in the nude across the corpse-carpet.
Unroll your tongue across the battlefield, exhale life
from that holy hole, through those pearline teeth.
Ingest us, your Pureness, process us, excrete us.

But for now, let down your air, your Highness, save us
from the offal we've fallen into, from slumlords' swampy
rumps and gush your cosmic colonic, flush Auschwitz,
taunt Laura Mulvey with your vapidity, your gaze-absorption.

There is no purity but you are pure, there is no air but you have air,
there is no sanctuary but you are a safe church.

Quintessential

Her personhood
throbs in her ankles,
earlobes, her bush.

Who says the honed
eye is this- or that-phile?
That anatomical parts
are interchangeable
carrots on fetish sticks?

For a time, the entire
woman can be found
in the jugular notch,
on each fingertip
and buttock freckle,
those humid thighs,
philtrum, plantar fasciae.

A lifetime's footprints
mark a path over
the mown or foresty
isthmus between the
two most private orifices.
Lick her Nth-Wonder-of-the-World
teeth and taste biography.

She, the beloved,
the unrepeatable,
the woman within
and without, is an
atomized monarchy,
each part a sum of
her whole.

I nuzzle umbilicus, clavicle, nipple and whisper, "You. You!"

Untitled, or Untainted

Scatalogicians say "we're born between urine and feces"
and evolutionists reduce human births to fishy non-events.

I rebut that we burst from Zeus' head and correspond
to true love as the moon reflects the sun.

We are one part piss and shit, three parts magic.
There is a vast heaven between the hole and the hole.

Part 5:
"Yours Truly, Mathematicus"*

*O austere mathematics! . . . You gave me the coldness that
exhales from your sublime conceptions, free from passion.*
— Lautreamont, *Maldoror*

*You see, I believe so completely in the life of a human being
and the sanctity of a human being.*
— Martha Graham, *Blood Memory*

All this is horrible, but it is history.
— *The Last Day of a Condemned Man*

* *alleged Jack the Ripper signature*

Iago(s?) of Whitechapel

Jack of many names.
Saucy Jacky. Jack the Ripper. Mathematicus.
The Whore Killer. The Beester. Jack the Riper Ar Ar.
J.T.R. George of the High Rip Gang.

His letters were signed "From Hell," "Dear Boss," "Believe me ever."
His knife was "a treat," Queen Victoria a whore he buggered,
"ripping up a dear creature" a thrill for this true-life Spring-Heeled
Jack: the gleeful hunter, snuffer and ripper of women.

Was the Ripper a *he*, a lone wolf of dank, carnal Whitechapel,
or a *they*, or a press- or prankster-mustered name and persona?

Unlike Hitler, Stalin, Manson, and Jim Jones, he doesn't seem
to have been a loser with a bone to pick with planet Earth, but,
like the Bomb, he was a deft show-off, a self-delighting Iago, an ego
exulting in clever dastardy, mischievous manipulation, tearing apart.

Saucy Jacky was the usher of the World Wars, the pope of serial
killers, the muse of Nazi doctors, BTK, Gary Ridgway, Joel Rifkin, Hutus.
Whatever, he was the last fact of life seen by whores Mary Ann Nichols,
Annie Chapman, Liz Stride, Catherine Eddowes and Mary Jane Kelly.

(Don't accept lesser concern for murdered prostitutes, for there's a
sacredness to these tough entrepreneurs, a preciousness and power,
their control of the lust-sewer endorsed by both Augustine and Aquinas,
their honesty in this facade-world impressive, their deep, deep humanity.
Judge not! Magdalenes deserve the same defense as queens.)

So, was there a single Jack, or Jacks at random, copycat Jacks?
Did he/they rise from a lower or upper stratum?
Aren't the infamous letters sensational bunk?
Is there one Jack, or two — or more?

Sure, most of the letters are hoaxes and hysteria-pleasers, but are they
any less Jack: the true killer who channels humans' common demon?
His/their sick words are incense that wafts up from The People's temple.

Look to your left, look to your right, look up, down.
Yes, every letter is genuine, no matter who wrote them.
Yes, there are one and many Jacks: master races, commie Man-Gods,
bombs, utopian butchers, feral hippies, the Jim Joneses next door.

Mary Jane Kelly

You and Sharon Tate were about the same age when you both met your torn dooms: her, the snuffed star, and you, the most mutilated of the Canonical Five Ripper victims, defaced and gashed beyond belief, skinned to bone, literally robbed of your heart, poor "Ginger."

Why do I mourn you most? Why does the horror seem more horrible? Were you saved to be the last of the ill-fated chosen because you were blue-eyed, fair-haired, younger, cute and reportedly clean (so portrayed by the cream of the celebrity crop): a breath of fresh Her, a slum Bardot?

You outranked the rank and foul Daughters of Joy whose sticky thighs were fat lips around Whitechapel's livid and veiny collective sin-meats. Their bodies were sewage ballasts while yours (though frump-destined) was a pack of Lucky Strikes passed through a war-bent infantry.

I tell myself that your looks and hygiene don't matter, that my especial shock is at your mutilation's severity, the incomprehensible savagery of the assault that is best described as a ritual tantrum, an *erasure* of a person.

But I haven't a tenth of the shock for the others: the rundown, unkempt *miserables* who appeared to have no business making their bodies their business, who lured clients by some miracle rather than worthy attraction.

You were a treat though, weren't you, Marie Jeanette, Limerick lass, white sheep of the family? Swept through rank Whitechapel like a baby's first exhale: more like a fallen star than slum destined tail, a whore. Mourned most by me (though God bless the others).

If Looks Could Be Killed

Is death a hottie-hating reverse-eugenicist?

Did the Ripper knife favor the rundown whores
for their closeness to dissolution, as if good
looks approach completeness, signify more
intelligent and worthy design, as if the so-so
and ugly rub elbows with the grave's fragmenting
decay, the humus' oafishness, and don't need as
much preparation for festive worms' sloppy seconds?

Mary Nichols, Annie Chapman, Liz Stride and Catherine Eddowes:
their missing teeth, their older-than-they-were aspects,
their pitiful physiques fooled the knife into believing
that their bodies were halfway dead anyway, so —
though ruthlessly — it undid them with less vim than
it did Mary Jane, the one rose of the bunch, because
she transcended death's subtractive math, was
assembled more ingeniously, quenched mens' leers
with implicit evidence against the law of fundamental
entropy and said, "I'm fair despite unfairness, I glow in
muck and sweeten the night. I'm *this* despite all *this*!"

Did the good-looking whore die worse for her looks?

How the Ripper knife must've shook with the desire
to cancel her desirability, to trample the petals, to
topple the sculpture, vandalize the edifying face that
was DNA-eons in the making (as savage tribes deface
artwork and piss on shrines), punish genetic primogeniture,
make a molehill out of a mountain, tar and feather
Bouguereau and Rubens beauties, decrown all queens.

The Ripper: Molls of Whitechapel

My *noms de guerre* are Jack the Ripper,
Saucy Jack, the Beester, Mathematicus.

I hunt Whitechapel, I hunt Spitalfields:
the joy toilet, the hive of whores.

I'm a spy in the house of molls.
This is the Joy Division, baby.

As if a herald for my coming, that harlot cholera
tramped these death-deserving streets.

Cholera choked the living shit out of these
peasants who were nothing but living shit.

Reckless Abaddon (Apollyon, Destruction) blows through
cities from era to era, swallowing Sodoms, toppling Babels.

Mark me, however: this is no puritan crusade,
no act of righteous vigilantism.

It's pyrethrum, precaution, grassroots sanitation,
an epidemiologist's war against future Big Stinks.

Whores are walking sewers with no outlet,
no egress into the dark-lady Thames.

Chuck Dickens and his utopian reforms couldn't
redeem *Oliver Twist*'s Nancy's sold soul and hole.

(Oh, Moab's and Midian's daughters will perish
and their blood will mingle with the dumb dust.)

No, Nichols, Chapman, Stride and Eddowes is not
a law firm. No, and again no. It's a lousy cliterati.

Mary Nichols got a smile carved across her neck, from
ear to ear, and my knife minced her crinkum-crankum.

I knife-noosed Annie Chapman's neck then nicked her
uterus and bladder, part of her cunny — her belly button.

Elisabeth "Long Liz" Stride sucked a breath mint while I spun
my web, so her carotid artery freed a fragrant rainbow.

I spared Eddowes' quim but her uterus and kidney were on
my shopping list. (I sent the kidney to Mister Lusk, from hell).

(Who will be blamed for everything, down to the lowest whore-
meat? The Jews, of course. They're never not blamed.)

For my swan song, I rest my predacious roving finger
on the mother lewd, the cream of the crotch.

Mary Jane, you will know that I am the Lord.
Oh, fairest Daughter of Joy, merry Magdalene.

I'll savage your body into Something Else which
will burn its image on humanity's retinas, hot slut.

Those with the same scorpions in their hearts, those
touched by Factor X, will emulate my handiwork.

Know what the coroners will sing at the inquests,
my moll madonna? "Like a Surgeon!"

They will know that there was no glee or "release"
involved: only the grimmest ripping.

They'll photograph your gashed and jellied
head: your true face relegated to sketches.

Under my microscope and scalpel, prime specimen,
the sole truth, death, is exposed for worship.

Against all fairy stories, scriptures, gospels, love
pledges and sermons death is a deafening aria.

No godly light dispels shadows, blind-faithful fool.
No critic pans the carnage-art of my sharp "brush."

Shudder and wring hands, righteous bystanders, but
you admire my street art, my unapologetic installations.

You'd love to unleash your imaginative wolves
and turn other-flesh into your whim's slave.

Look at the look on Gustave Dore's illustrated Red Riding
Hood in her devoured grandma's bed with the satyr wolf:

Her eyes both scared of those claws but also curious,
even expectant, precociously glimmering lust.

Some perverts long to be eaten alive by a careful
cannibal, to be gobbled like Saturn's sons.

The thrill of diminishment by a famished other's teeth:
all women secretly want to be a beast's feast.

My knife is hungry, Mary Jane, it wants to dine, Mary Jane.
Mary, I'm the New Cholera, the canny cannibal.

Sing "A Violet from Mother's Grave," you drunk slut.
When I end your song, Kelly, don't fear the Ripper.

As Riding Hood was saved from the wolf's belly via Caesarean
section, I will rescue your heart from the desecration.

Ladies, Exist Again!

Mary Jane Kelly, marijuana namesake, you're impervious to your
ejaculating Johns and ripping Jack, you transcend Whitechapel's
actual and human sewage, the killer's sharp, brutal kisses.

Torn woman with legs apart,
the post-mortem report on
your remains rings with a sound
poetic, its morbid description
as complex as the cannabis plant.

The plant: angular, resinous pubescence, acuminate leaflets, basal
leaves, petals, stamens, axillary and terminally germinated flowers, fleshy
endosperm and the seed hugged by a shiny achene's curvy embryo.

The woman: legs agape, left thigh right-angled at the trunk, right thigh
obtuse-angled at the pubes, abdomen and thigh surfaces removed,
viscera emptied from the abdominal cavity, breasts sawed off, arms
mutilated, face hacked away and unrecognizable, neck tissues cut
to bone, uterus, kidneys and a breast cushioning the head, other breast
near the right foot, liver between the feet, intestines on the right, spleen
on the left, removed abdominal and thigh flaps piled on a nearby table,
skin and tissue between the costal arch to pubes cut away, butchery of
the right thigh down to the bone, vagina, and right buttock. Heart missing.

"I hardly recognize myself," Marie Antoinette once wrote in a letter.
Mary Jane, I can't help but hear those words echo from the Tuileries
Palace to your Dorset Street hovel: who *could* recognize you after
the Ripper's ecstatic art — let alone you?

Antoinette wrote two words
in a letter to Count Fersen
before the shit really hit
the hand fan: "I exist."
Oh, bloody Marie!
Oh, bloody Mary!
Exist again!

The Ripper: The "Dear Boss" Letter

[The blood] went thick like glue and I cant
use it. Red ink is fit enough I hope ha ha.
— The Ripper?

I'm down on the whores.
Only my arrest or death will save
them from Jack's nimble, quick rip.

ha ha

I laugh like a machine.
No, I *write* a laugh like a machine.
My "laugh" is light from a dead star.

A true laugh lives in a sudden
outburst, in an avalanche of guffaws.
Someday symbolic emotions will replace real ones.

ha ha is a laugh-mask hiding
a humorless diabolic: I know mirth as well
as I know Grover Cleveland or Victoria's dirty secrets.

Have you ever tried to write in blood?
It goes thick like glue but shoots quickly
from whores' arteries as if crimson ejaculate.

ha ha

Whores' sins lurk in their furry places, in their
vulgar mouths and fishy dollymop-slits,
poison and pickle their lying hearts,

It's all that fast food and booze,
the infused breath and goo from johns
who need to poke the muck of human blindness
once in awhile to "keep it real" and demolish their idolized
selves far from the eyes of wives, priests and reputable business.

There's a perfume that siiiiiiiighs out when the skin's unzipped.
I prepare a meat feast for silent bacteria and clicking insects.

Who's Smarter: Mary Jane Kelly or Condorcet?

Marquis de Condorcet, utopian cheerleader
turned victim of the ripping French Revolution,
believer in liberal progress and human perfection
even when it was his turn to face Saint Guillotine
(he died waiting in prison), was named — get ready —
Marie Jean. (Sound familiar?)

The whore chose the finer, truthful route, Condie.
Your Enlightenment's Rousseauean/Reason-children
were weapons of math destruction.

Part 6:
Charlie Manson and the Scorpion Children

The law of the tiger's temperament is, Thou shalt kill; the law of the sheep's temperament is, Thou shalt not kill.
— Twain, "The Turning-Point of My Life"

Woman, I'm your friend . . . We have graves to dig.
— Sam Minard, *Mountain Man*

I shall come, I shall punish, the Devil be dead.
— W.H. Auden, "Danse Macabre"

Susan Atkins: Something's About to Go Down

Shhh.

You hear that?
Not the desert wind,
not the swinish snores
of our dreaming Family.

That. Hear it?

Something's coming.
Something witchy.
Something's about to go down.
Something we were born to do.

Shhh!

There it is again.
Crawling like a king snake over bones.
Something coming, about to down.
A fertile sire, the father-load!

Do you hear it? Do you *hear* it?

Why are they sleeping through this dawn before Dawn?
We should be spreading Love — without mercy!

Let's rise and shine!
We have shit to do!

Charlie: Man-Son

My children (my scorpions) sleep.
They are my reflections.

Prophets drift in from deserts, live in deserts.
Ministries spring from waterless places.
This dusty ranch is a spawning pool.

My scorpions (my children) stir within
my waxing belly. They crave birth.
Death.

August 9, 1969

Los Angeles: fame's shameful streets, bronze men, slutty mansions.
Ghosts of sins crawl the Hills, stomp the Valley, the Canyon.

Scum come down from the Haight, the Ashbury, hunting new highs,
harvesting hippie chicks' bony nakedness with cult-slick tongues.

Those duds, that bud, Ken Kesey's bus of blown minds, these things
are for the mere moment: trivial, brief dust, wisps.

There are other things afoot that will carve deep into time.
That led to this. This came from that. Evil is a perfect flow, a beeline.

Who told us this horror tale? Who but the horrormakers themselves?
Sharon Tate's fate is known only from the murderers' tongues.
Even so, it's all we can rely on, as if clinging to razors.

*10500 Cielo Drive, Benedict Canyon. A hot, muggy summer
morning. The Polanskis' maid arrives at the house. Sharon Tate
rises from bed an hour later and spends some time poolside.
Folgers Coffee heiress Abigail "Gibby" Folger and her boyfriend
Voytek Frykowski are already gone. Gibby purchases a yellow
bicycle and arranges to have it delivered to the house later in
the day. The strained lovers return for lunch then leave again.
Gibby goes to a psychiatrist appointment during which she
seems to hint at an eventual breakup with Voytek. Two blue
steamer trunks that Roman Polanski sent ahead from England
arrive in the late afternoon and are placed in the living room.
Hairdresser Jay Sebring drives to the house and answers the
door when Gibby's bicycle is delivered. Gibby and Voytek re-
turn later in the evening, and everyone goes for dinner at the El
Coyote restaurant on Beverly Boulevard. When they return to
the house, Gibby gives her mother a phone call and then settles
in bed to read while Voytek enjoys some music on the stereo
near the living room and Jay gets stoned while chatting with
Sharon in her bedroom.*

*Not very long before midnight, young Steven Parent parks his white
Rambler in the driveway and visits William Garretson who has
been staying in the Polanskis' guest house about 100 yards from
the house. Parent returns to his car a little after midnight.*

As Parent prepares to drive off the property, Charles "Tex" Watson, Susan "Sadie" Atkins, Patricia "Katie" Krenwinkel and Linda Kasabian drive up to the gate. Tex cuts the phonelines, and the group walks toward the house. "Suddenly, that whole section, number 10500, was cut out of the rest of the world and lifted into another existence," Atkins will later testify. "We were separated from the whole world. Perhaps for the first time in my life I was deeply aware of evil. I was evil." Tex hurries over to the Rambler's driver-side window and kills Parent. He then climbs into a side window of the Cielo house and lets Susan and Patricia in while Linda stands watch outside.

Voytek is asleep on the couch in the living room. Tex wakes him. "Who are you?" groggy Voytek asks. "I'm the Devil," says Tex, "and I'm here to do the Devil's business." He ties Voytek's hands together. Susan checks the hallway, is waved to by Gibby, then runs outside to get a knife from Linda. After retying Voytek's hands with a rope Tex brought, she herds Gibby, Sharon and Jay into the living room.

Tossing a rope over a ceiling beam, Tex ties Jay's hands with one end and wraps the other end around Sharon's neck. When Jay protests, Tex shoots him through his left lung then kicks him in the face. Jay attempts to escape by crawling away, but Tex stabs him again and again in the back, kicking his face again and again. Voytek tackles Susan, who stabs him in the leg but loses control of him. He then breaks for the entrance hall and Tex pursues and tackles him, they roll into the steamer trunks and somehow Voytek keeps going toward the front door. Tex's gun blasts Voytek's back and right leg, then it backfires so Tex leaps onto Voytek, cracking his skull with the gun and stabbing repeatedly. Blood laughs everywhere.

Linda runs down the driveway toward the house when she hears Voytek screaming "Help me! Oh, God, help me!" and he bursts from the front door, looks directly at her then pitches forward into a hedge. Tex pounces on the ragged, mewling meat and finishes him off with the knife, stabbing and stabbing until his wrist sinks into the jellied guts, the gore, the nothing Voytek has been reduced to. "Make it stop!" pleads Linda as Susan exits the house. "It's too late," Susan answers fatally. (Garretson claims that he didn't hear any of this from the guest house.)

Inside the house, Patricia is shocked to realize that Gibby's
hands have become free of their bonds and Gibby makes a run
for it until Susan reenters the house to help Patricia: "I give up!
Take me!" Gibby groans (in some unwitting, macabre language
of sexual surrender). But the body receives the message much
later than when the mind writes it, so she manages to break
away again and staggers out of the door near the kidney-shaped
swimming pool — only to be overwhelmed by Krenwinkel who
chok-chok-choks her belly and chest with the knife. "Stop! I'm
already dead!" Gibby cries. This pitiful plea only serves to alert
Tex to the need for more butchery, so he takes over the machine-
like stabbing with absolute glee.

When Susan returns to the living room, Sharon begs to be spared
for the sake of her unborn child. "I want to have my baby! I want
to have my baby!" What mighty power breaks through the utter
awe of being before an earth angel — especially one bulging
with fetal life? How can there be no real devil when human scum
transgress not only the chivalric law but the law that beauty
must survive, must be smitten only by age or natural causes,
that the very angelic DNA deserves preservation and should
cause the would-be transgressor to drop to his or her knees in
mid-attack, change the murder course as Hamlet did when he
saw that his loathed uncle was kneeling in prayer, and weep
at the almost-crime?

Susan will later testify her total lack of pity for Sharon. "You're
going to die, and I don't feel anything about it" are probably
the last words Sharon hears. She never ceases her whimpering
and pleading until Tex and Patricia return and Tex swipes his
knife across the left cheek of Sharon's nevermore-to-stun-a-room
face. Both Tex and Susan commence ripping in and out of her
with their knives, the squish and slosh among the dying woman's
screams and gasps — until Sharon blurts her final words, her
pitiful, heartbreaking "Rosebud": "Mother! Mother!" Susan will
say that the stabbing felt "better than climax," that it felt as if
her knife was "going into nothing, going into air," a feeling like
an orgasm mounting with each knife slorp into Sharon's body
which was so beautiful they could pray to it. Standing before
the warm ruin of a woman, the emptying heart quietly noisy,
Susan considers removing the living fetus but there's no time.

Before leaving, Susan dips a towel into the Sharon-mess and wipes the word "PIG" on the front door. "I was the living death," Tex will later say. "I wasn't alive anymore," Susan will say. And Krenwinkel: "I was very dead inside."

The next night, the same crew (sans Linda, plus Leslie Van Houten) slaughter Leno and Rosemary LaBianca. After Leno is stabbed 26 times, Tex carves "WAR" into his belly. Rosemary is stabbed 41 times. Glowing in their art, the murderers shower and help themselves to food in the refrigerator.

"But the horrormakers told us this tale! How do we trust it?" Oh, I believe it went down almost exactly as it was reported.

When pride brims in sinners, they become open, accurate diaries. "But Susan Atkins called prosecutor Bugliosi's case the Magic Motive!" Oh, the Bugster knew his shit, but his version of Manson is too tall.

When the first chapter begins with peace and love, expect a bloody end. That led to this. This came from that. Evil is a perfect flow, a beeline.

And the human heart, in turn, flows from ecstatic carnage: enlarged, engorged, enlightened in the majesty of the fundamental anger of the flesh.

Charlie: "I Have X'd Myself from Your World"

While in prison during the trial, Charlie carved an X
(which later became a swastika) on his forehead
because he'd x-ed himself from the world.

In 2004 a *New York Times* promo for CBS' *Helter Skelter* movie
featured Manson *sans* swastika: its X unhooked, castrated.

Maybe they x-ed the swastika to spare us the symbol
that conjures Buchenwald, snaps at eyes like piranha.

Serial-killer Dennis Rader a.k.a. BTK (Bind, Torture, Kill)
blamed his sexual murder on "factor X," which only
stops when its host is jailed or dead.

Malcolm X x-ed out Little to manumit his name from
"the blue-eyed devil" — also to defy the Beatitude
that promises the meek the world?

Hero Zorro ("fox") leaves a mark that's half-swastika
(the better half), and dull Christians mistake the Chi-Roh X
for a removal of the Christ child from Christmas.

In 1945 a 1910 self-portrait of a noseless, mouthless Hitler
was found: his lonely initials and an X above his head.

X marks the damned spot.

Creepy Crawl

We.
Creepy crawlers
creepy crawling.
We.
While you sleep.
Crawl.
While you're not home.
While you're home.
We.
Float on the dark:
spidersnakes.

Turn TVs toward walls,
rearrange and steal.
You don't know we
were here. You know
we were here.
We are here.

We.
Creepy crawlers
creepy crawling.
We.
Walk like penguins
in the tricky dark.
While you're not home,
while you're home.

We.
See your secrets.
We.
Could slit your throats.
Stab your guts.
Eat your leftovers.
Pee in your milk.

California Dreaming

The Mamas and the Papas' John Phillips heard
something in the house and left the bed to check.

In the dark he saw barely visible people dressed
in black, waddling like penguins.

Back in the bedroom, Michelle told John to tone
down the drugs and pop a Valium.

Once John said that the Polanskis' pool glowed
in the yard "like a giant turquoise stone."

Charlie: I Am That I'm Not

I am you and you are me.
I birthed you and you birthed me.
I am the white, you're the yolk.
You're the shell, I am the hatchling.

As my crawling king snake makes you
bleat, bitch, I roar, "I AM THAT I'M NOT!"

If you think you have a choice or
even have a name, wandering jewel,
you put Descartes before the whore,
honey, because all of us are holes
that lead from nowhere into nothing.

As my staff draws cold stone from warm
water, bitch, I roar, "I AM THAT I'M NOT!"

You were born and I died.
You died and I was born.
Your legs have been open
lifelong to shame daddy dearest.

I am every demagogue who has eaten The People.

Bitch bleating: "Ohmygod, are you my god?"
Me roaring: "I AM THAT I'M NOT! I AM THAT I'M NOT!"

Leslie Van Houten: "Every Day Was like Halloween"

When that Beach Boy Dennis Wilson kicked us out
of his pad we rolled on over to Spahn's ranch and got
down, *real* down. I mean, there was no beginning
or end to our flesh, it was like one big crawling animal
with no mind, with no name, with no end to its appetite,
without a brain or a sober bone in its body.

"Bow like sheep," Charlie'd say, and we'd all get low,
real low, and grunt like animals, with knives strapped over
our dirty panties, smashing our abyss-mouths together
to suck the rank darkness, while Charlie watched us
crouching and grunting in nothing but our stinky panties,
bowing like sheep: grunting, mindless, filthy for him.

Every day was Halloween and everybody was nobody,
anybody, in-synch animals, disembodied bodies glued
together by love and stink and Charlie.

David to Young Leslie: *Here I am, Stinker Bell, girl with a skull earring!
Here I am to lay my life at your dusty toes and turn the knife's handle
toward you, to trade my life in exchange for theirs: the souls whose
guts sizzle for Molochs, Man-Gods, your animal Halloween.*

Leslie Van Houten, Stinker Bell

> *The only fuck I want right now is the orgasm*
> *of the great fucking grave.*
> — Jim Jones

Me:

Recede your wet fuzz, Leslie.
I'm not the nothing or nobody you seek.
Leslie, I can't have sex with death.

Those brainy rook-black hot psycho eyes,
those daddyless longlegs that spread like
the Bottomless Pit for Rosemary's hell-sent
baby daddy to swallow her white Slippie
antichrist like the pissed-off blackie night.

Young Leslie:

"Buzz buzz *goes the orgy,* ring ring *go my bells.*
Honey, grab me before I surf the next stink-wave.
Buzz buzz goes the orgy, ring ring *go my bells.*
Who's who, his or hers — who cares? I'm an
ever-replenishing pie, a pilled pillow of happy-holes,
the Queen of this be-alive hive, so dare the wet-fuzz
forest, have sex with death."

Me:

This is how I think of you, though you've grown old
in prison, have reformed a thousand times over,
mentored and excelled, added to the AIDS Quilt —
no matter how many college degrees you can get
and sincere apologies you can give, denied parole
is all they'll give and all you'll get (unlike some wrist-
slapped Nazi war criminals), and I share the blame
for keeping the girl with the hot psycho eyes alive.

This resistance is a ruse, Leslie.
My righteous disgust conceals the skull's approving grin,
the Thanatotic magnetism and die-curiosity in us all.
Do I desire the LSD-lubed Stinker Bell over the current penitent?
Do I crave sex with death, and does the gallows shadow over
our bodies turn and spur me on?

Old Leslie:

She's still in here, honey, and she's dying *to get out.*
Look deep into my old eyes, past the reforms and kind tone.
She's in there!
Look harder.
Harder — harder!

The Devil in the Details

My whole life has been decided by fate.
— Sharon Tate

Fate happens.
— Aristotle Onassis

It's bad enough that Anton LaVey, founder of the Church of Satan, played the Devil in Polanski's *Rosemary's Baby*, but Manson's association with Thelemite/Crowley crony/Church member Kenneth Anger, filmmaker of *Lucifer Rising* and *Invocation (of My Demon Brother)*, added to Sharon Tate portraying the ravishing but Satanic Odile de Caray in J. Thompson's *Eye of the Devil*, makes Salem's past witch paranoia seem sober, especially when you know that Manson-fan Bobby Beausoleil played the role of Lucifer in *Rising* (the original prospect, a five-year-old boy, had died after falling through a skylight — not unlike how the film's luminous namesake fell from Paradise). Bobby, who knifed Manson Family friend Gary Hinman, sociology Ph.D hopeful and peace-loving Buddhist, to death and left a bloody "paw" print because Charlie Manson needed to implicate the Black Panthers because he mistakenly thought they were after him for shooting "Lotsapoppa" Crowe, a drug dealer who'd been ripped off by Tex Watson and mistaken as a Panther. Bobby, who Truman Capote called him a "Forty-second Street Lucifer," who jammed in a rock band called Love, whose surname means "beautiful sun" in French.

Hinman, that credulous, idealistic wimp, bled to death while chanting "I devote myself to the Lotus Sutra of the Wonderful Law" before his Buddha shrine, while losing his life at peacenik hippies' hands, living the death that Beast Crowley's Madame Blavatsky promised: the iron justice of the Law of Karma, delivering the same jaw punch that Marquis de Condorcet must have felt when his beloved French Revolution sentenced him to the guillotine — though he wrote praises to humanity's "limitless perfectibility" until he died in prison while waiting for his turn at the chopping block.

Sharon, staying over at former-fiance Jay Sebring's 9860 Easton Drive (once home to Jean Harlow, whose hubby Paul Bern, an MGM producer, shot himself in the head — or so it goes), awoke to hallucinate a "creepy little man" near her bed and fled to the stairway where she saw another man with a gashed throat tied to the post. The future blabs itself to us non-stop, people, and if we'd just shut up and listen, we won't be so surprised when our respective Reapers interrupt our silly paths and say, "Fini your best-laid schemes, mice."

Sharon and faithless but ingenious Roman Polanski, survivor of proto-Manson Hitler and director of *Repulsion* (starring Tate-level beauty Catherine Deneuve and lots of knife/blunt-force violence), of *Knife in the Water*, of *Cul-de-sac* (starring Deneuve's sister, in an isolated castle atop a mountain), moved to one of Rudi Altobelli's properties, the former residence of big stars such as Michele Morgan, Lillian Gish and Cary Grant and last lived in by Candice Bergen and Terry Melcher (Doris Day's son): 10500 Cielo Drive (Sharon called it "the love house"), high up in Benedict Canyon, L.A., like an isolated castle atop a mountain, overlooking Babylon. Cielo means "heaven." (So much for foreshadowing.)

Terry Melcher left his pet cats behind when he and Bergen moved, so kind-hearted Sharon made sure to feed them and their descendents — twenty-six cats in all — daily. (She was butchered to death at age 26.) Melcher: the dork who bagged model/Abbie Hoffman-groupie Bergen and produced the Beach Boys, the band that starred Dennis Wilson, who was Melcher's ride back from a tour of the Mansons' Spahn Ranch commune — a ride back to Cielo Drive, a ride including none other than Charlie Manson, who rapped his knuckles on the front door of that same house a year later, after Melcher and Wilson flaked on a recording promise, and was told by guest Shahrokh Hatami to "take the back alley" after assuring him that Melcher didn't live there anymore, so he tried the guest house where Altobelli (who later sued the Tate estate for the carnage-caused property damage) slammed the door in his face. Sharon saw Manson (and he saw her, imprisoned her image in his eyes, for sin is in the eye), and she asked Altobelli if "that creepy-looking guy came back" on a later plane trip. (Don't forget the "creepy little man" at Easton Drive, Sharon!)

Remember Beausoleil, Satan role-player and Love guitarist? He was imprisoned for the Hinman murder, and Charlie, scared that

he'd roll over on him to make a deal, needed to pin Hinman on
the Black Panthers to exculpate Beausoleil: hence — Susan Atkins
was later adamant about this — the Tate/LaBianca murders were
born. Beausoleil told Truman Capote in a San Quentin interview
that Sharon and gang pissed off people with bad dope deals and
were far from innocent. Voytek alone probably had more aveng-
ers after him than can be counted on two hands. (This is why
Sharon's father, Paul, questioned folks such as Mama Cass, drug-
gie Steve McQueen and drug-pal Billy Doyle.) Bobby bullshitted
that "everything that happens is good," and when Capote asked
him if that included war, starvation, pain and cruelty, Beausoleil,
Love's "beautiful sun," said, "Whatever happens, happens. It's
all good."

Stanton LaVey, son of Anton, called Manson "our own mes-
siah" and told Marlin Marynick that nothing was random in the
murders by the Family — down to the very time. "Tex did not
make a mistake," Manson said. "There's no such thing in my
kingdom." Filmmaker and Kenneth Anger pal John Aes-Nihil
rejects coincidence, that the Manson and Tate circles were
familiar ("everyone knew each other"), celebs slummed with
hippie bums: porous Cielo having been a laxly public party pad
and who knows what else (Dennis Hopper claimed S&M). Gregg
Jakobson, Dennis Wilson friend and Manson admirer, let Fam-
ily member Dean Morehouse (father of Ruth Ann Morehouse,
Family member who loafed on Temple and Broadway with
"Squeaky" Fromme, Sandra Good, Bobby Beausoleil's buddy
"Gypsy" Share, et al, during the Tate/LaBianca trial) stay at the
house between Melcher/Bergen and Polanski/Tate. Bums such
as Tom Harrigan and Pic Dawson (bestie with Mama Cass and
drug dealer to both Voytek and Sebring) were regular partiers
there. And guess who swam in Cielo's kidney-shaped pool? Su-
san Atkins, the Manson girl who would be tempted to cut the
living fetus out of Sharon's corpse's belly, who said the bliss
of stabbing and stabbing was orgasmic (Anton LaVey guessed
that the crime was "a lust murder," that the knives imitated
sex), who dipped a towel in Sharon's blood and wrote "PIG"
on Cielo's front door because Charlie said to "leave a sign,"
"something witchy." Oh, they were in their wits and had volition,
because Charlie wanted the deed to be deliberate, and, since
(like antichrists Bormann and Himmler) they were worse than

their master, their alleged dissociativity was due to bloodlust in human sharks driven wild by human chum.

Yes, Manson didn't point to Cielo on some roulette wheel, but ordered Tex Watson, Susan Atkins, Patricia Krenwinkel and Linda Kasabian to do the devil's business "where Terry Melcher used to live." How is this any different from Hitler's international tantrum born from interminable frustration, mediocrity, post-war shame and the back-stabbing Versailles Treaty? Once an obscure loser in a Munich crowd then making Neville Chamberlain his Brit bitch in the same city twenty-four years later, every sleepless naught remedied by infinite war, impotent rage channeled into blitzkrieg, gas, ovens. Or, for you vampiric *literati*, "Take the back alley" is like young Thomas Sutpen being told by the house negro to go to the back door in Faulkner's *Absalom, Absalom!*: that discovery of shame fuelling his lifelong (and thwarted) ambition and his regular scraps between "wild negroes" — as if lacerating the memory of that humiliating day.

Finding his Fifteen Minutes between the Yippies and the Yuppies, Manson, lord of what he dubbed the Slippies, took Abbie Hoffman's outrageous admonishments to the next — actual — level, as director John Waters observed. Waters, who dedicated *Pink Flamingos* to "Sadie, Kate and Les" (Susan Atkins, Patricia Krenwinkel and Leslie Van Houten), had drag-hag Divine refer to Sharon in *Multiple Maniacs* and dedicated *Female Troubles* to Tex Watson. Charlie went back to the Polanski house to assess the success of the killing floor. Imagine the car taking them higher and higher, toward the literal and figurative mansion on the hill, up and up: the low places rising like backed-up sewage to the high places. Ascend, scum! Thrust yourselves up, crustaceans! Rise, rise like the bone-turned-weapon from the world's first murderer in Kubrick's *2001*, rabble! Rise, rise, lowlifes! Crawl from the obscure streets, the anonymous desert, storm the palace and slay the Queen and her privileged court!

Was Roman mixed up in some occult soul-selling? Did he portray key elements of his wife's bloody future in a cinematic past? For instance, filming *Rosemary's Baby* at The Dakota, the place where John Lennon was gunned down by Satanic Mark Chapman (John Hinckley's unwitting mentor). The Beatles, Manson claimed — oh, he didn't believe his own bullshit! — used their *White Album* to subliminally endorse Helter Skelter, the ultimate race war in which blackie would rise up and slaughter whitey *en masse* until blackie fucked it up — as blackie always does — and the savior Mansons would crawl up from the Bottomless Pit to grab the reins and make it work — as whitey always does. According to Charlie.

The Beatles (who hail from Liverpool, home of the famous art gallery, Tate Liverpool, of all names) probably stayed at 10500 Cielo Drive back when Melcher and Bergen lived there (Lennon conflated it with Doris Days' pad since Melcher was her son). The band might have known Ken Anger and been courted by or involved in The Process, the occult church that gave Manson the Bottomless Pit idea and the melding of Jehovah, Lucifer and Jesus, the church that might've inspired Sirhan Sirhan to kill Bobby Kennedy, brother-in-law and lover to Jackie O., whose look-alike "cameoed" in *Rosemary's Baby*'s Satanic rape scene (when Rosemary was impregnated by hell's seed) and married criminal/Kennedy-nemesis Ari Onassis (who cursed Camelot at a Haitian voodoo ceremony — not knowing that Bobby owned an Onassis voodoo doll).

"Then have your killing," Jehovah declares in The Process' Robert DeGrimston's *Jehovah on WAR* ("WAR": what Patricia Krenwinkel carved into victim Leno LaBianca's fat belly the night after the Cielo Drive massacre). Sirhan Sirhan was imprisoned at San Quentin while Bobby Beausoleil was there and spoke to ever-curious Truman Capote, who wrote *In Cold Blood* — which Sirhan claimed inspired him to self-entrance via mirror-gazing as one of the killers in the book had done — and saw Theosophical fingerprints at the crime scene. Truman's third-to-last dying words, as Joanne Carson — yes, Johnny Carson's wife — claims, were "Mama, mama." (Sharon's last words were "Mother, mother.")

Imagine the grief of Doris Tate, Sharon's mother, when she heard the grisly news of her daughter's death. Doris, who, worried sick over her daughter's relocation to L.A., told her psychologist that she felt that Sharon would be attacked or murdered over there. Her fear came true in a nightmare about a cowboy pointing two guns at her and Sharon in the Cielo living room and announcing, "Today you will die." Dream-Doris fled but realized that Dream-Sharon couldn't escape the mad cowboy and had been murdered on the couch.

Nine Inch Nails founder Trent Reznor lived in the Polanski house and named his recording studio Pig, after the bloody word Atkins left on the door (the door he later relocated to his new Nothing Studios), and a sign on the door read "COME IN HERE AND BE KILLED" the night of his housewarming party, which was attended by Butthole Surfers' lead singer, Gibby Haynes, whose first name is eerily the same as murder victim Abigail "Gibby" Folger. What was recorded at the Pig studio? Marilyn Manson's (ahem!) *Portrait of an American Family* and Nine Inch Nails' *Downward Spiral* albums.

The Mansons (such a warped portrait of an American family) had lived in a Topanga County house they called the Spiral Staircase (which shares the title of a Robert Siodmak film about a woman-terrorizing serial killer), a place probably once owned by a Church of Satan disciple, but they relocated to George Spahn's ranch, which had been used as a town set for King Vidor's *Duel in the Sun*, a film starring Jennifer Jones, Joseph Cotten and — can you guess? — Lillian Gish, one of the many former celebrity residents of 10500 Cielo Drive.

Star-News Headline: "Film Star, 4 Others in Blood Orgy"

> *Gun sales rose extremely in the two days following the murders. Expecting the worst, Steve McQueen, a fellow partier at 10500 Cielo Drive and one of the names on a Manson Family hit list, carried a gun until the fear dwindled.*

Guns for sale!

Don't relegate yourself to the tooth and nail!
Do you *know* what a real punch is like, to get or give?
No sound effects or instant knockouts: it's like rock
against rock, a two-by-four against rubber.

But a gun levels the peasantry and the elite, the frail
and the giant, the Girl Scout and rapist, knife and flesh.
It high-speeds the verdict, skips the clauses, races sound
and wins, pisses off would-be despots, gives assailant
scum that shocked jaw, that "Oh, shit!"

Guns for sale!

Don't listen to those faux pacifists who advise ducks to tremble
under desks in terrorized "gun-free zones" rather than admit
that that's as sensible as desk shelters during nuclear blasts.
Heavenly hosts don't descend while devils pause to reload.

Guns, not dogs, are defendants' best friends in a pinch.
A holster under a dress is the best thing in the new Old West,
a bullet in the chamber is the most precious metal on Earth.
Do not reject the Dirty Harry within, citizen, or you'll go extinct.
Conquer death with death.

Guns for sale!

The Regina Killers

Wow, they sure are beautiful people, thought Susan Atkins
when seeing Sharon, Jay, Voytek and Abigail for the first time
on the soon-to-be killing floor in the living room of the insular
Polanski home (called the "love house" by Sharon).

Goodnight, Jay. Goodnight, Gibby. Goodnight, Voytek.
Goodnight, Sharon. Goodnight, goodnight . . .

How else could this mouse girl react after she'd been acclimated
to the Manson aesthetic that shunned showers and glorified orgy reek?

Imagine the powerful awe when Sharon's panicked flop down
on the couch still seemed like a danseuse's *tendu* to *fondu* and
sexy Tex seemed an ape next to debonair Sebring.

What does a knife do best but disassemble what seems fearfully
and wonderfully made? Our viscera are truly aesthetically equal
so why not turn these could-be-models inside out and say fair's fair?

Goodnight, Jay. Goodnight, Gibby. Goodnight, Voytek.
Goodnight, Sharon. Goodnight, goodnight . . .

Later, Susan assured the recipient of a confessional letter:
"Those people died not out of hate or anything ugly."

Patricia Krenwinkel: Tex Isn't Human

The man on the couch wakes up and asks Tex what time it is and who Tex is, and I want to tell him that *I* don't even know who Tex is because his voice has changed and become all guttural, and it says, "I'm the Devil, and I'm here to do the Devil's business."

We have never been so sober, so alive, so thrilled and with it! I dedicate every one of my body's cells to the law of lawlessness! Mother, if you could see me now: I am become living death! God, if you see me now, I am one with your crucifixion!

The other man, the one Tex shot and kicked in the face, is trying to crawl away and Tex sticks his back with that knife again and again, kicking his face in and laughing like a new creature, a non-human thing, an all-hunger, the Bomb.

Abigail "Gibby" Folger: "I'm Already Dead!"

The suffering gets under your skin.
— Abigail Folger on social work

I bought a yellow bicycle this morning. Earlier this evening
I told the shrink that I'm sick of Voytek's shit and I want out.
Phoned Mom while stoned (I still can't hide it from her)
and snuggled up with a book in bed, under that tacky
stuffed rabbit mounted on the wall.

Then, after midnight, I wave to a familiar mousy hippie girl
who passes by my bedroom door. She returns with a knife
and forces me into the living room where a handsome but
beastly man and a girl who looks like Peppermint Patty are.
(Have they partied here, swum in the pool, sold us speed?)

Voytek's hands rope-bound.
(How can I ever leave him now?)
Jay strung up to the ceiling beam,
as helpless as a feather.
Sharon scared shitless on the couch.
(That silly U.S. flag draped over its back.)
"You are all going to die," says Beast
in an inhuman voice.

Suddenly Voytek (my man — Voytek, I wouldn't have left you!)
crawls like a squashed spider toward the front door until Beast
dives on him and they crash into two steamer trunks that Roman
sent from England. Beast shoots him twice and cracks his skull
(it sounds like a frozen lake breaking) with the gun. His knife:
shk shk shk shk shk shk! But Voytek (my man, my man forever,
for we're all going to die tonight!) lunges out the door and Beast
follows like a flood with Mouse behind while Peppermint Patty
keeps watch and I hear a girl outside beg Mouse to "make it
stop" and Mouse says, "It's too late."

Sharon pleading on the flag couch.
(Her pregnant belly shiny-tight,
her panties, sweaty thighs.)
Jay a heap of silent, dying stillness.
(Heard them laughing together earlier . . .)
Voytek outside pleading for helpOhGodhelp.
*

(Part of me resents him, wants to spit at his
blubbering fear, his inability to save us.)
Old Glory indifferent behind terrified Sharon.

Then suddenly: freedom! An angel of absent God loosened
the rope and I run until Peppermint Patty tackles me and Mouse and
Beast burst back into the house, so I let myself crumple, hearing
myself say, "I give up, take me" — amazed that anyone, let alone
me, could sink to such a point of despair, to say "take me" to her
killers, the spillers of her lifeblood, the thieves of her existence,
and Beast stabs away at my flesh: *spat spat spat spat spat spat!*
The best part of waking up is Folger guts to cut.
We're all livid on a yellow bicycle, yellow bicycle, yellow bicycle . . .

Beast stabbing like a machine, perfectly,
in and out: we spasm together, like sex.
(His noises are happy, like a nursing animal's.)
My face! The knife slashes across my face!
(My head feels lighter, as if it's disappearing.)
This is happening to *me*, to my body since birth!
It's not *my* body or *a* body anymore — I'm sliced baloney!
And Mouse looks at me as if staring at a blob.
(*My* daddy could buy *your* daddy. Yeah: Mr. *Folger*,
bitch, as in the coffee emperor — but you win anyway!)
Voytek shrieks again, luring Beast back outside.
(Thank you for the distraction, my blubber-pussy man!)

I sprint to Sharon's bedroom and Peppermint Patty avalanches
behind as my blood runs away from me — then I'm trapped under
her and the knife becomes a powerful piston: *chuk chuk chuk chuk*
into my chest and *slorp slorp* into my stomach, and I'm amazed
again at what I hear myself say: "Stop! Stop! *I'm already dead!*"
I'm alive to report that I'm already dead!
This is real and happening to me.
I can't stop my blood from coming out.
My body (not "my" — I *am* a body!) is beyond help, beyond repair.

It's my birthday in two days.
Born August 11th, died August 9th.
Ashes to ashes, August to August.
Phone mom.
Rabbit.
Sharon belly.
Shrink.
Yellow bike . . .

Ears That Hear

An eerie home video was found: Gibby, Voytek,
a man named Witold Kaczanowski and a Jane Doe
stoned and dining on roast before the Polanskis' fireplace.

Gibby reminiscing about when Voytek had once
seen "a blazing pig's head" in the same fireplace,
the microphone left near the roast all the while.

So there's a recording of the carving, of knife against
bone, drowning out their voices with each loud cut.

"There were no words," said Linda Kasabian, who stood
watch as Gibby and Voytek burst from the house in their
bloody, futile tries at escape. "It was beyond words."

After the dying died down, Susan Atkins dipped a towel
in Sharon Tate's blood and wrote "PIG" on the front door.

People, We Choose Our Poisons

1)

Born-hack artist Valerie Solanas shot through Warhol's
spleen, liver, lungs, stomach and esophagus with a
.38 snub-nosed revolver.

After he blew off the script she gave him, how did she
avenge her bruised (sh)ego? Fed his *oeuvre*: awarded
him a motif for his popular gun screenprints.

2)

The CIA trained and supplied the mujahideen, which became
sentient and came back to sting the programming hand.

3)

When Lt. Helder named the Mansons as prime suspects,
Roman Polanski pooh-poohed, "Come on, Bob, you're
prejudiced against hippies."

Sharon Tate thought that hippies were "great" and only
wanted niceness and peace.

4)

Public-opinion obsessed Louis XVI bashed the crooked
rich while aristocrats frothed in-vogue class frenzy only
to fall prey to the angry masses.

The reform-enamored king reconvened the Estates-General
and appeased his way to the throne for necks: the guillotine.

5)

National Socialism wasn't a reaction to the corrupt Weimar era,
it was a product — offspring — of it, its rotten fruit.

Henry Ford's *International Jew* was a domino that knocked Nazi
Baldur von Schirach and Hitler toward the Final solution.

6)

Maybe we don't *choose* poisons, but we secrete them, and they burn or sicken us: a regressive version of Fred Hegel's dialectic spiel.

"Nature is acoustic," Soren wrote. "Heed what the echo answers." Man-God Manson liked to say that "the question is in the answer."

Charlie: "I'm a Boxcar and a Jug of Wine"

When Charlie realized that Dennis Wilson and Terry Melcher had been disenamored with his strum-accompanied rants, he decided to fashion his own audience and consumer base through myopic entrepreneurship: fashion an echo chamber (self-ignition validates bored firemen or Reichstag "defenders").

While Wilson was still Charlie's dupe (he called him "The Wizard") and indulged him with a recording, Charlie's repetitive "digh de day" turned into "die today, die today, die today": an age-old preface to the final solutions of epic losers who strike out when up at bat and decide that the game's score should be zero/zero.

Five-foot-two Charlie stands with platform-shoed Stalin and Kim Jong Il (whose Godzilla knockoff, *Pulgasari*, portrayed a doll that grows with every quaff of human blood). Charlie wet-dreamed of rising to the powerful shortness of Macedon's Alex or Napoleon. No wonder writer Ian Fleming wrote that James Bond "mistrusted short men" because they are the cause all of the world's trouble.

A year before the Tate murders, Valerie Solanas, *SCUM Manifesto* author and butch gendercidist, was pissed that Warhol ignored and lost her *Up Your Ass* script, so, deciding that he should pay in blood (she was an unknown artist who deserved fame, after all!), she shot up the Factory (killing Andy for a minute and a half).

Charlie's guitar was like Solanas' barren pen (replaced by her Warholocaustic revolver) and the sterile brush of "little corporal" Hitler, painter of amateur landscapes, who deserved rejections from Vienna's Academy of Fine Arts. Everyone knows that mite makes Reich, so Charlie Man-Son, decided to be unborn.

Bernardine Dohrn, 1969: "The Weathermen dig Charles Manson." Charlie twenty years later: "I'm nobody."

Sharon Looks Up at Her-Hair-Like Sun

I want to
Don't want to
Why am I?

There's so much
Too much.

I have to
Tomorrow
Where will I
Next year?

Not enough time
Too much time
Baby kicks.

He touches
And *he* touches
They touch me
I cry.

We're all alone
Love, where are
Cats shun.

I'm known from temples to ankles only.

Movie stars
Highs
Shave legs
Baby's coming.

Light candles
Read to repel skulls
Swim from fears.

My heart is so loud
This castle's evil
Son, son, love, come

Is the sun dying?

The Baby Lived Twenty Minutes After Sharon's Last Breath

Sharon, my fate awoke
when it felt your hot shot
blood and witnessed the
Helter Skelter abortion.

To protect you from the devil's
businessmen, to redeem your
body pregnacious from the
fin de Sixties bellicist hippies
is my highest dream.

"I want to have my baby! I want to have my baby!"

You begged those soul-midgets
to take you to their lair and kill
you after you birthed your son.
The gleeful stabs that replied
seemed to make the one girl cum.

I don't know when it hurt
most to look at you: when
you glowed alive, or when
you smiled slightly and stupidly
in your gurgling gore.

My fate awoke when it felt
your hot shot blood, heard
your final "mother, mother"
and the shriekless fetus in
the Helter Skelter abortion.

"I want to have my baby! I want to have my baby!"

Davidus the Doubter Keeps It Real

Secret between strangers?
I'm no hero.
All this Bogart is smoke.

I'm full of shit.
How can one *not* be in this global toilet?
We live in *anus mundi*.

I preach my lip-sermons about the power
of poetry against Tienanman tanks, of art
against berserkers, chivalry against rape.

But the worthiest lovers are sundered:
Cleos and Tonys, Rhetts and Scarletts,
Abelards and Heloises, Sams and Dianes.

Poets are mute before guillotines, quake
before Inquisitors, become blank pages burned
by Red Books, books devoured by academicians.
Speechifying wannabe heroes talk themselves to death.

Rousseau, who, like a stopped clock, was right twice
in a lifetime, said that the act of writing slays the plenitude
of presence — so should I snap my pen in half?

To fight the shit
I've built myself into Bogart,
a holographic hero.

I light a cigarette,
flick the nihilist off my shoulder
and declare war on the anus of the world.

(God, save me from the Abyss!
God, God — God save the Queen!)

Davidus Prepares For Thermidor

Multitudes can't contain me.
I'm an abyss that doesn't look back.
Everything I see is a scene, is Louvreable.
I see in slow-motion, slow you all down,
X-ray spectacular: you can't hide the hot spots.
The Cool makes this blind man see — deeply.
The Cool makes dandies into knights of faith.

I am strong in the aphorism and the power of its might.
I'm sent into the bloodbath as war correspondent,
as witness to men's cannibalism of men, to warn
others of the Third World savage in all three Worlds,
to intercept trigger-words designed to activate atrocities.

But shouldn't narrators of horrors be messengers who shoot?
After all, bullets, not flowers, stop devils. Guns, not prayers,
are penicillin. Or is the nonviolent resistance a tank to flatten
all Panzers? Or is the best offense a turned cheek, penance?

Is the kiss the indubitable answer to Inquisitors?

Davidus Thermidor Visits 10500 Cielo Drive

You can't undo something that is done.
— Leslie Van Houten

[O]nly where there are graves are there resurrections.
— Nietzsche

I can't stop the winds,
tame the scorpion,
command tectonics,
woo the wolf.

Ladies beg me: "David, stop the rippers' knives."
Gentlemen urge me: "Drain the bloodgutter."
Pro-lifers cheer me: "Go and kill death!"
My wife pleads: "Stay with me, and let the world go to hell."
My mother: "Never believe in the grave."

I can't stop the plague,
evaporate tsunamis,
untwist tornadoes,
quell the killer bee.

Shadow of Light, you put me here to do something, to explode
the plans of the Evil One, to dam the blood flood. As a child,
I felt a heroic will, a Robin Hood urge to swing and save damsels,
to avenge stolen virgins, to plug gun barrels with pimpernels.

Can I repel the rapist,
counter the headhunter,
swindle the cheat,
outwit the suicide bomber?

I can't tolerate one more lost life, one more unanswered plea
for help, one more unrealized salvation, but I'm no superhero,
though I prayed to be one since childhood, so please descend,
Light Shadow, and mend my spirit's apartheid, integrate me.
Burn the despot tarots that have predicted only doom for me!

Is my outrage born from foreseeing
my own demise rather than altruism
for butchered victims? (Do all our
dramas end in bloody final acts?)

In *The Grand Design* Stephen Hawking and Leonard Mlodinow estimate the existence of 10^{500}th universes, so I march forth in defiant denial of time's restraints and forward-onlyness, taking a sideways leap of fate, intent on iterating the infamous Tate event in another dimension with a Herrlean plot rather than the only one we know, the one in which banal devils win.

I swear that "Sweet Jane" means
sui generis *and reverse time-work*
inspires life ex nihilo, *restores*
Tates and Antoinettes!

Those laser-sharp physicists just may be on to something: imagine an Etch-A-Sketch that retains and remembers every willy-nilly knob turn or excruciatingly planned powder-scratched Rembrandt: each universe earning permanent placement in a cosmic Library of Congress once an idea is jotted or a slightest move is made.

How does that world-famous
toy work but by pushing away
the grey to expose the
underlying darkness?

In *It's a Wonderful Life*, George Bailey's youngest daughter, Zuzu, shows him her treasured flower, and when some petals fall off she implores her distressed father to do the impossible: to perform a miracle and "paste it," to reverse entropy, perform restoration.

Zuzu, Zuzu, go to sleep
and dream, dream
that your healed flower
has become a garden.

1943: Livchitz, Maistriau and Franklemon ambushed an Auschwitz-bound train and freed seventeen out of 1,618 Jews, inspiring over two hundred more to escape. The men were caught and killed, but they'd defied fluxing history, tried to paste a broken flower.

Who You Are, grant me the power
to heal Zuzu's petals for real,
to rescue every *prisoner from*
that hell-bound train!

I look out on the infinite spaces and tremble as Pascal trembled. Doubt and anxiety rise in me when I regard nature's manifest denial of I and Thou, Shadow of Light, so save me from Darwin and Skinner, from tooth and nail, let me earn my stripes, don a cape, heroize!

Give me August 9, 1969.
Let me into the fin de Sixties.
Let this be restitution for Queen
Antoinette, for ripped Mary Jane Kelly.

That night: Sharon stabbed sixteen times; Jay stabbed seven times and shot once; Gibby stabbed 28 times; Voytek shot twice, beaten 13 times and stabbed 51 times. A week later, Aquarian children united in universal love and peace at Woodstock.

Peeking through the cavern's narrow chinks has turned me into the loneliest man on the planet, a migraine for my wife, an insane raver in an airless, deaf wilderness. But look on I must, or my madness will be cured by a madder Pollyanna madness, an ignorant bliss.

The world is fire, the human heart is fire,
the law is fire — so be like water, life-water:
unbruisable, unstabbable, babbling or
roaring, rage like water against the fire.

Who You Are, bless me with the Cool needed to fool my enemies. Send Unununderstandable Peace, Restless Restfulness, the wintry summer, the subzero fire. Hide my face behind my true face, the face you knew before my birth, before love made me.

POET, APPROACH THE GUILLOTINE.
SURRENDER YOUR HEAD TO THE BLOCK.
TRUST COOL CHRISTMAS AS THE BLADE THROWS YOU
FROM TIME'S ORBIT, FROM TODAY TO THAT NIGHT.

Here I am: a Psalmic Eeyore who renounces gloom, girds my tail with a bright ribbon and plunges faithfully into the Hundred Heartache Wood. How do I save them? Blow off the devil's businessmen's balls? Or *hug* them to death?

I CREATE IN YOU A CLEAN HEART,
I RENEW YOUR DOUBTFUL SPIRIT.
*

I SEND TWO ANGELS TO AID YOU.
YOUR TONGUE IS YOUR WEAPON.
CHRISTMAS IS MY FOOTPRINT.

Move me from bone-freezing snow to the stinky heat of L.A. summer.
Keep the Bomb from obliterating mercy, from igniting vengeance.

WAKE UP FROM WAKING UP, DAVIDUS.
BREATHE IN THE STINK OF THE *FIN DE SIXTIES.*
GO FORTH, THERMIDORIAN PIMPERNEL.
(REMEMBER THE LOFT. THERE'S HELP FROM ABOVE . . .)

I awake standing on the threshold of the Polanskis' living room.
It's a hot, sticky night. Tex Watson has just shot and stabbed Jay
Sebring, and Sharon Tate is sobbing on the couch. I'm a little
late. Voytek Frykowski is struggling to free his hands and Abigail
Folger seems frozen in shock. Patricia Krenwinkel and Susan
Atkins stand by, waiting for orders from Tex.

"Who are *you*?" asks Tex, clutching his gun. "And where did you
come from?"

I feel a sheathed sword on my back. Reaching back and touching
its hilt, I know who I must be. "I'm . . . the Scarlet Pimpernel."

"The scarlet pimp *what*?" Tex growls. Forty years from now this
scared overgrown boy, this dead-spiritual brother to these three
girls made witchy by this world's toil and trouble, recalls that he
thought he was "an animal" of the Apocalypse, the "living death,"
on this August 9th night.

I glance up at the loft that runs parallel with the couch and has
a small wooden ladder leaning against the edge of its right end.
There's a small room or closet up there too. I smile inside. The
loft is part of this drama, I remember that much. But it's not yet
time. "The Scarlet Pimpernel. Sophie Scholl. The White Rose.
Thermidor. Thermidorian Grey. I'm shaking history's Etch-A-
Sketch and turning its knobs to redraw this drama. I'm pasting
the petals on Zuzu's flower. It's elementary, my dear Charles
Watson."

"Tex, what'll we do?" Susan Atkins asks. She looks at me as if I'm
a ghost — which I am.

"Hello, Sexy Sadie," I say.

"How did you know that name?"

"Shut the fuck up, Sadie," Tex spits. "Don't talk to him." He raises the knife and gun as he steps toward me.

"They're going to kill us," Sharon whimpers. "My baby, my baby!"

I feel a saintly smile ripple onto my face from within. "Nobody is killing baby Paul, Sharon," I assure her.

"*Shut up!*" Patricia cries, almost dancing with nervousness.

Voytek is about to make a break for the front door, but my arm shoots up. "Not now, Fry," I say. "Relax. See if you can help Jay."

I flash my eyes at Abigail. "Gibby, console Sharon." The coffee heiress obeys, seeming not to care who the hell I am and where the hell I came from. Tex is shaking in his madness. He'll tear me limb from limb if I lose this Cool.

"Your leader is dead," I announce, stepping toward Tex with outstretched arm and open hand.

Patricia: "Charlie's *dead*?" Susan: "He's a lying shit!" Voytek: "We need to call the police!" Me: "I *am* the police, Fry."

"*You're* the dead man," growls Tex. Lunging at me, he stumbles and falls forward to the floor, dropping both the gun and knife. I snatch up the gun and kick away the knife.

"No, I'm not lying. Your leader is dead. He's been dead since you met him." I unsheathe the sword and point it at the girls. "You slept with a corpse, mated with a mummy." Looks of absolute understanding of my meaning drop like shades on their faces.

"*Kill you . . .*" grunts Tex, rising. I drive the tip of the sword through one of his cheeks and pull it out in a blink. He falls back and howls in shock and agony. My eyes return to the girls as I withdraw the sword.

"They cut the phone line," Voytek gasps.

"No matter, Fry," I say. "This is as it should be: the house cut off from the world, isolated and floating in lonely space, past the point of no return to Earth like the spaceship in Kubrick's *2001: A Space Odyssey.*" Wondering if any of them have seen the film in the theater, I motion to Sharon and Gibby. "You okay?" They nod in unison, awestruck.

Tex continues to writhe on the floor. Susan and Patricia remain frozen. "He's out of his mind!" Susan whines. "Where did he come from?"

I glance up at the loft again. Nothing yet. Tex clenches his hands and kicks the floor. "I'm going to *kill* you!"

"Be polite, Tex. I have the mic now. Everybody put your patience caps on, because it's time for a Galt-long lecture." I touch the sword's tip to his other cheek. "Where do I come from, Susan? I come from a long line of fools: of artists, dreamers, pacifists, philosophers, optimists, humanists, humanitarians. We're either sterile cowards or destructive meddlers. What has history taught us but that the poet is mute before guillotines, the warm-blooded mystic defers to the frozen scientist, the sage is the cremated of the crop, Heideggers hail Hitlers, the martyr fertilizes evil flowers, pacifists become cannibals, humanitarians kill their fellow man to save their fellow man, dreamers slumber during massacres?

"Whether through complicity or complacency, we fools feed or neglect the rotten cultural rabble and evacuate figurative thrones in favor of enthroned vacuums. Ineffectual moongazers are corpulent in word but waifish in action and don't heed the 'go' in Logos. They mope like ignored prophets or wrap themselves up in hollow hopes and toothless tropes, or they strum lyres while barbarians barbecue Rome! Meanwhile the poison trickles down or up, from the evil rich or the evil poor, from puppetmasters or mountain-levelers, from militants or tiny twerps-turned-Big Brothers. Necessary authority ossifies and justice-seekers become lawful gavels refashioned as despot hammers.

"Beware especially of the artists. Who is more dangerous than the disappointed or thwarted artist? Blue periods give way to bloody red ones. Back in your parents' day Baldur von Schirach, a failed poet and artist, was appointed Youth Leader of the German Reich and head writer of lousy Nazi anthems by that era's Manson, Adolf Hitler — who was an aspiring painter and filled his study at Berchtesgaden with books on painting and music. Wasn't Goebbels a hack novelist and Goering an art collector? Wasn't Mao a poet? Jean-Paul Sartre, who praised 'irrepressible violence' and *praxis* via 'mad fury,' mythologized butcher Che Guevara. And Che transcribed Neruda!

"Destruction is usually justified by apparently altruistic and 'peaceful' goals. Humanitarians created the guillotine. Opponents of capital punishment beheaded Antoinette. John Lennons become Vlad Lenins who exceed Czarist brutality with flying colors. Puritan Cromwell was an ethnic cleanser. Reverend Malthus and Darwin's cousin kick-started eugenics. Hippocratical doctors abort and euthanize. Einstein and Manhattan Project scientists doomed Hiroshima and Nagasaki. Antichrist Hitler wrote that humaneness and aesthetics become irrelevant in a state of emergency and beauty ceases when the humane and beautiful goal is threatened. Ugliness preserves beauty. War is peace. I'm sure you hippies have thrown around the term 'peace' a lot. Most bellicists do. I fear the wager of peace as much as I fear the wager of war.

"Massacres, democides and genocides tend to be utilitarian in nature, paved with good intentions, based on humane manifestos. Foolish angels outnumber crafty devils. If it were possible to round up the out-and-out evildoers, the sickos who maim, kill, pillage and destroy for the rush alone, there'd be a surprisingly small crowd. Violent instinct rarely reigns on its own. It's usually rationalized or staggered into by a much larger crowd: so-called do-gooders, humanists, humanitarians. Almost like clockwork those who claim to champion the people decapitate the people in order to 'save' them, or perform 'just one more' necessary purge before the pure are free to perform their restorative work. The optimist welfare-state of Nazi Germany looted the very people they called lice and rodents. Egalitarian coups inspire inequality. Saviors of the peasants feed them famines. Peacemakers are often the Grim Reaper's best friends. Your Family was *based* on peace and love! You didn't *join* it for war and hate! And where has your hippie peace and love led you? Into 10500 Cielo Drive to do the devil's business! Which *brings* us to your dear leader, your dead sire, your Charlie 'No Name Maddox' Manson."

Both girls seem to flush with sudden boldness and strength. "Don't you talk about Charlie that way!" Patricia growls.

"You mean the man who feeds you that horseshit about Helter Skelter, the Beatles' *White Album*, a worldwide Negro revolution and the Bottomless Pit? *He* doesn't even believe it! His trip is much more purposeful, scorpion-children, much more personal."

"Don't listen to him," Tex grunts. "He's a liar."

"What would think of your desert guru if I told you that the blood on your hands flowed from Charlie being a hack musician? Most demagogues and Man-Gods have fallen short of record deals, so to speak. Homeless Hitler moped obscurely while the magnificent worlds of architecture and art swayed far above him like Olympian gonads. No wonder the loser resented the cultural and commercial prowess of the 'capitalist Jew.' Unrecognized artistry and an unrealized record deal: not exactly Hercules strangling snakes in his crib. Another typical banal evildoer. Nazi Adolf Eichmann wasn't a foaming-at-the-mouth berserker guzzling Jewish blood and orgasming at the sight of gassed masses, but a squeamish man who claimed to be a cog rather than an autonomous actor.

"Simply put, your dear leader is a Beatle wannabe. Everywhere Charlie turned in his desperate quest for fame and rivalry with the pop-culturally well-hung Beatles a door slammed in his face, not by cold and intolerant bigwigs, but by himself. Though the music industry and even Hollywood courted him, his dupes eventually realized his banal flaw, and he spit in the very eyes of the people who were willingly blind to his crimes and bullshit. No matter how far from his wretched origin he ran, he was tracked down and beaten by self-hatred. Like young Hitler, he tramped the streets, waiting for a miracle rather than refining himself. Assaults and battery don't train such losers to bob and weave, they just build calluses around their hearts, and then the bums mistake the calluses for armor and reckon themselves righteous knights on singular quests for fate-ordained success. They find other crustaceans who long to coup against Atlantis, who are tired of the status quo and need an illusory reboot. But these losers are losers despite the cults or wars they start. Behind callus-armor quiver thin-skinned runts who covet actual attractants, envy genuine progenitors, effectual creators and Perfect Ten beauties.

"You saw Charlie kiss Beach Boy Dennis Wilson's feet at their initial meeting, and temporarily bewitched Wilson let you bums shack up at his pad until your bullshit and STDs made him kick you out. But were you in the studio when Charlie made a fool of himself and proved to *not* be the promising star he thought he deserved to be? Were you there when he bugged the shit out of Rudi Altobelli and Terry Melcher even after it was evident that they wanted nothing to do with him? How about when he thought he'd murdered Lotsapoppa, who'd been mistaken as a Black Panther, and shit his pants with worry over imaginary Panther retaliation, so he used the Helter Skelter mumbo-jumbo to prime the Family for violence? You surely were at the ranch when his eyes finally looked down the path of no return, when a lifetime of degradation compelled him to lash out as the wild animal he claimed society turned him into.

"What do you think that was all about? Ushering in a Negro murder spree that would act as a cleanser on this anemic reality, leaving a clean slate for your superior culture and race? You didn't see that everything he did was to pamper and save his own ass? You didn't see that his hip and 'together' exterior barely hid a bumbling schemer who masterminded bloody capers rather than tight heists and cool coups? You didn't see that the dwarf's legs are stilts? Every self-crowned End All, every cultural and cult hack has a big bone to pick with someone — or with the world at large. Some are pissed that the bread lines don't line up in front of their compassionate kitchens. Some resent that voters don't want or need them. Some want to be the very rich that they claim to despise. These desperadoes who level mountains and raise hells are actually nobodies — and spread the virus of nobodiness with their scorched-earth tantrums. Know what philosopher Hannah Arendt called bureaucracies? 'Rule by Nobody.' And who are you ruled by, Charles, girls? A fake wizard behind a curtain. A Pompeiian lava cast.

"*Nobody* draws up globe-sized programs and arbitrates the rules. *Nobody* tours the towns and preaches that *his* elixir is the elixir of elixirs. *Nobody* needs perpetual injustice to validate perpetual reform, perpetual inequality to promise equality — and the power to scrap everything and everyone if reforms and promises fail. *Nobody* sparks and prolongs the wars. Zeros establish Year Zeros. It's the drive toward non-being, the salmon-swim back to pre-primordial non-waters before This and That, before *before*, as if Love never birthed Light and inklinged each of your unique faces and counted your hairs."

I gesture at Gibby, Sharon and Voytek. "They are far from innocent, maybe even far from decent! However, however: *so* precious, *so* priceless! The slightest fired neuron is a unique star in boundless space. A wax-master Madame Tussaud may be able to replicate the outer glory — but never the inner. Scorpion-children! Don't you see that every murder is a Bomb of infinite megatons? The Etch-A-Sketch shakes, the cosmos disintegrates, the Bomb gobbles gleefully, the famished vacuum feeds."

I wave the sword from left to right as if squirting them with a hose. "The saving disgrace, scorpions, is that you're the minority, and your kind burns itself out. You haven't the masks and costumes of philanthropic meddlers to hide and prop you. You're the easiest to snuff because you stand out like sore thumbs. There'll always be a Batman, a gunslinger or a swordsman who'll wipe you out. Zorros are greater than zeros."

I raise the gun and the sword. "Teddy Roosevelt said that 'you can't get peace from peace.' Only big sticks protect soft words. I use the sword and the gun so I don't have to use the sword and gun. But know this, Charles: there can be no outward peace if there's no real peace within. Nothing comes from nothing."

Tex stops groaning on the floor and growls, "*Why* are you telling us all this?" Susan, Patricia, Sharon, Gibby and Voytek look on as if waiting for a straightforward answer to the same question.

I check the loft again then readjust my grips on the weapons. "Because I owe this lesson to you. Because love isn't love if it doesn't love the unlovable. My own heart weeps for yours, and the heaveny part of me wants to hug all of you until the ice melts — though the Bomb in me wants to erase you from history altogether, to torture you without restraint or rest."

Suddenly I become dizzy, and the stench of collective sweat be-comes an intoxicating fragrance. *"What grade do we get if we've learned your lesson?" Susan says in baby talk. The way she narrows her eyes and slides her tongue at me makes her more attractive than I ever could have imagined. Her body twists like a snake neck beneath her sweat-wet clothes. Patricia, the homeli-est of the girls, becomes as alluring as Sharon herself. The girls grope each other, their eyes drunk with self-debasement. This must be a show they do for Charlie back at the ranch whenever his whim blows. He owns them, pulls their strings, tells them who to sleep with, when to grunt like animals, when to cook and when to kill. "You sound too much like a preacher, teacher," Patricia pants. "Sit in the corner with us bad girls, forget all that book-learning." She licks Susan's lips.*

Tex and Voytek are kneeling in prayer, their eyes closed and wide smiles on their faces as they mutter "We devote ourselves to the Lotus Sutra of the Wonderful Law" over and over, as if praying before execution. The girls fall into an animal kiss un-til Susan detaches and waves her arm over Sharon and Gibby. "You came here for these two, didn't you, dirty boy? Well, take them. And take us. We'll call Linda in, too. The more the mer-rier." As if on cue, Gibby slides down to the floor and kneels before Sharon, worshipping the shiny belly. Her nightgown rides up. Sharon's head lulls back and she grits her teeth in pleasure. "Oh, I want it, baby," she groans, "I want to have it, baby . . ." The toes of her worshipful feet claw at the shirt on Jay's back. I hear Jay gurgling "Die today, die today, die today" from a blood-filled mouth. The rank sweat smells wonderful. Gibby stands and lets her nightgown fall to her ankles like a dropped white flag of surrender, and Sharon reaches for her greedily. Then Charlie Manson himself steps to the edge of the loft and grins down at me. "Doesn't all that shit you know and talk you talk make your head hurt?" he asks. "No more teaching, preacher. Take them! Force them to bow down to you like sheep. Love them as you love death. Taste their stink, drink their spit. Feel their surging life before we slit their political-piggy throats." I feel myself go anything but limp and step toward the writhing sluts, and I —

Jay lets out a horrible sound and breaks the spell. "Is he dead?" Sharon shrieks. She nudges his back with her foot. "Jay! I think

Jay's dead!" I recall a famous photograph of the two of them pos-
ing outside the house: Sharon in a maternity blouse and a bikini
bottom and Jay in nothing but cotton briefs, his starkly outlined
penis like a flaccid exclamation point for the life-affirmative YAWP
of her baby-full belly. Then I flash to the most infamous grisly
crime-scene photo of them: Sharon's right arm flopped over her
head, her left hand balled in a rigor-mortis fist, her blood-soaked
bra and panties, rope loosely tethering Jay to her like a mockery
of an umbilical cord, both corpses in fetal positions.

I shake my head at her. "I'm sorry, Sharon. I awoke too late. But
nobody else will die. Isn't that right, Charles?" I hold the sword
tip against his throat.

"Ye . . . yes," he grunts. "*Shit.* Yes! Untie them, Sadie."

"But, Tex, he might . . ."

"*Just do it!*"

With shaking hands, Susan loosens the rope around Sharon's
neck while Patricia undoes Voytek's bonds. "Thank you thank
you thank you," Sharon runs from the couch as soon as she's
free. Gibby shakes her head in shock and relief.

Suddenly the door behind me opens and I swing around, draw-
ing the gun while keeping the sword pointed at Tex's throat. It's
Linda coming in from outside. Her jaw drops when she sees me.
"Please don't shoot!"

"No worries, Linda," I say. "Come in a stand by your sisters."

She obeys and shrugs at Tex. "I swear I didn't see him come up
the driveway, Tex."

Voytek starts to pace as if ready to explode. "We need to get the
police up here right away!" I almost reach for my cell phone
and then realize that it's 1969, when "cells" are biological and
penitentiary things only. Anything could happen in this isolated
house, so I need to maintain this Cool. I glance at the loft. Still
nothing.

"So, now what?" pipes Gibby.

"Are you going to let us go?" asks Susan.

"Not until my people are safe," I reply, sheathing the sword and covering Tex with the gun. Nodding to Voytek, I say, "Get them out of here, Fry. There's no phone line so get to a neighbor's house — anywhere else." He nods back, and smiles gratefully at me. When he looks down at Jay the smile is torn from his face.

Sharon stops and kisses me on my mouth. "Thank you, whoever you are," she whispers. Her lips taste like snot and tears. Her breath reeks.

"B-b-big fan, Sharon," I stammer. "*Big* fan. Take care of yourself."

They leave. We wait in silence for few minutes. The loft above is silent as a coffin. Suddenly Tex's demeanor changes. He seems to heal suddenly, to grow. "As the pretty lady in the nightgown asked before, Grey Pimpernel: *now* what?" He grins like barbed wire and rises from the floor. His cheek no longer bleeds.

"Careful, Tex," Susan warns.

I involuntarily peek at the loft.

Tex looks up there too. "What do you think's up there? There's nobody, *nothing* up there!"

He takes a step toward me. "This night, this house, this world, belongs to us. You've read a lot of shit, you know a lot of shit, you can quote thinkers and drop names — but where does it get you in the long run? Huh? You talk about beauty and mercy as if they're *things* we can touch and feel and grab onto, things that can move mountains." He shakes a fist. "But *this* is tangible and real! *This* doesn't think or talk, it acts! This is an immovable mountain. Think about what you've just done, Pump-her-rose. You made the very error you insulted and did the reverse of all those spy movies: orated so long that the villain got the upper hand! *You* plucked the lyre while Rome burned! This is why every bookworm who came before you failed to save the world. Words, words, paper-tiger words! Concepts, concepts, terminally-ill concepts! Your type says heady shit like 'This is not a pipe,' but guess what? Sometimes a pipe *is* just a pipe! We are what you see, man! There's no weepy baby locked behind my two eyes; Katie and Sadie are not lost girls crying out for help. 'War is peace?' Newsflash, poor little poet: Peace is *war*! We're the wrecking crew! We aren't aberrations, the underworld, the counterculture, a minority outnumbered by heroes. We're the majority — because we're *you* as well. We are *your* secrets and lusts that have grown limbs and escaped into the night. Your wettest dreams are realized in us. We are the lawless law of this world — and the world's true artists!" He gestures toward Jay's corpse. "And *that* is our poetry, our song, our sculpture!"

He takes another step — a stomp — toward me. "You want to know the bottom of all this?" The girls drift behind him, grinning and panting. "That whore. That perfect piece-of-ass living Barbie doll who owns this pad and all this nice stuff. A rich man's wife. Ever since Charlie knocked on the front door of this house, looking for Melcher, and saw her sitting by the pool, she stayed in his eyes. And when we first saw her she stayed in our eyes. Her image was all-consuming, like the old man's evil eye in that story by Poe. Except our blood didn't run cold, it ran hot, too hot to stand. And her haunting wasn't evil, it was sweet, too sweet to stand. We carried that glowing whore in our eyes, and she made us feel ugly and tiny. She was a perfect daughter, perfect sister, perfect wife, perfect mother, and we longed to slice her like baloney, to watch her guts spill out like boiled pasta. We wanted the million shards from her kicked-in glass castle to slash her body into meat-jelly. How fun would it be to shit on that perfect daughter, perfect sister, perfect wife, perfect mother? How could we get her out of our eyes once and for all, cool down our boiling blood? Rip her up. Kill Barbie. *That* would be the highest high. After all, there's no joy in obliterating the average or ugly. A fall from grace should be from a skyscraper, not from a fence or a curb. Kicking a pebble is nothing, dynamiting a mountain is bliss. Stomping on worms is no fun, but bringing down a giraffe or an endangered bird: now *that's* a party.

"Good enough analysis for you, Sickmind Freud? Are you envious? Can you say honestly that you wouldn't want to stab that whore at least once? You oppose me because I'm the part of you that scares you." He slams his fist against his chest. "Charlie Manson is *alive*. He's the part of me that I once feared but finally accepted. In every Charles is a Charlie; in every Charlie there is Charles." I think of the similar sounds of names and dooms: Charles Manson, Charles Watson. I grope for the Cool, but it seems to have blown away.

"You're going to let us go, right?" he laughs. "We *killed* a man right there on that floor, and you're going to let us go? Why don't you dare to exorcise us, defuse us, spray us with DDT? What good is mercy if it allows evil? What if we go somewhere else and kill even more people? What if I rape a child — or *children*? Then bury them alive? Whose fault will that be? Ours — or *yours*? How far does your mercy stretch? When should mercy defer to just aggression? You're conflicted, superhero! You hold a sword and gun but preach love and mercy. You weep for and want to hug us but also want to torture us without restraint."

"Tex, let's just get out of here!" cries Linda.

"Not one more word out of any of you bitches!" Tex screams. His head snaps back toward me. "Any other wise words to share, poet?"

I realize that the sword has vanished and the gun in Tex's hand again. The situation is beyond words. Appealing to scorpion-children is as futile as plugging a computer into a tree. I *can't* stop the winds, tame the scorpion, woo the wolf. Studies and concepts are noodle-swords. I'm no Pimpernel, no Thermidorian Reaction. I'm a Bogart made of mere smoke. Mute before the guillotine, the living death.

I look up at the loft one last time. Tex is correct. There's nobody up there.

"Come on, girls!" Tex cheers, handing them their knives.

Patricia throws her arms up. "Tex, he said Charlie's dead!"

"He's full of shit, Sadie. Everything he said is shit."

Tex kicks the top steamer trunk off the other one, opens it and spills out its contents: Sharon's clothes and a bottle of perfume that cracks against the brick corner of the nearby wall. The fra-

grance fills the room like a flash of light. The girls grip my arms
and waist. They push me out the door and follow Tex, who has
dragged the empty steamer trunk to an open section of the lawn.
He has found a couple of the gardener's shovels and passes one
to Patricia. "Help me dig."

"Dig what?"

"What do you think, Katie? A *hole*!"

Tex breaks the earth with the shovel. Patricia does the same.

"You don't have to listen to him, girls," I whisper to Susan and Linda.

"Shut up, you pig," Susan growls, jabbing the knife against my spine.
"You're going to die, so you'd better get ready." She dies of brain
cancer forty years from now. Her reform story is entitled *Child
of Satan, Child of God*. Her final word is "Amen." Tex becomes a
married father, an ordained minister and co-founder of Abound-
ing Love Ministries in prison. Patricia tutors illiterate prisoners.
Linda probably languishes bitterly in a trailer park.

Tex and Patricia are wheezing and leaning on the shovel handles.
Tex lowers the open steamer trunk into the pit, binds my hands
and feet with ropes then points downward. "Get in," Tex com-
mands. I slide into the cramped makeshift coffin and lie in a fetal
position. Tex latches the closed lid.

Will my daughter and son grow up to be artists or scientists, a
Sharon or a Susan, an Emerson or a Goebbels? What will my
wife think when she can't wake me because I died in my sleep
over half a century away? Forgive me, doll. Live happier, doll.
The scorpion-children cover the trunk with dirt and fill the hole.
I hear the indifference of the dumb earth. Die, David. De-lovely.
Shekinah shekinah shekinah.

———

I feel a peace that thought can't think, a wintry summer, a subzero
fire: Cool Christmas. It's like a blast of water from a hose on a
scorching day, like a wife's touch after a night of nightmares. The
fragrance of Sharon's clothes surrounds and soothes me. There
isn't much air left, but there *is* air left.

Then I hear faint, muffled voices from above: women's voices, not the Manson girls'. I remember the loft and (finally) the mission. I was told it'd be like this each time: as if waking from cryonic stasis, hazy at first. "David?" someone calls. "It *is* I, Maria Antonia, accompanied by Marie Jeanette. Are you alive and breathing?" It's the Queen.

"Barely, Your Highness!" I'm on the verge of gasping. "I hate to rush you two, but do you think you ladies can dig me out ASAP?"

"In a jiffy!" Mary Jane Kelly hollers.

I hear the dirt shift as the ladies dig urgently. My heart exalts upward and outward, and I remember more and more: who taught me to cheat time, who brought these ladies and me together, who taught us to say "no" to death. This burial was allowed to humble me, to teach me that talk can be cheap, especially when there's too much of it. There is an imperceptible door in this permeable physical system, eternity remedies infinity. *This* is the reboot: merely a brief descent then eternal ascension. There *is* someone in the loft. We can't solve it all on our own, but we're not on our own. Though our pastes fail and fail, Zuzu's petals have already been healed.

Then I hear the latches popping open, and the lid flies up. There's fresh air and light, and two lovely silhouettes. I sit up as my eyes adjust. "What took you two so long? You were supposed to back me up from the loft."

"We woke when we woke, David," Mary Jane says. "Then we waited to see what that muck-snipe and those glocky twists would do. At least your fakement succeeded, dinniit?" She uncocks her ivory-gripped 1911 handgun and slips it into a petticoat pocket. The Queen's stainless-sterling 9mm pokes out of her dress as if to introduce itself. I notice my sword is back, lying nearby on the lawn.

"So, they won't be bothering the LaBiancas tomorrow night, right?" I ask.

"We dropped a dime on them and warned the LaBiancas already," the Queen boasts. "And their camp will be raided shortly."

"'Dropped a dime?' My, my, Your Highness. You're quick with the slang!" I stand and hold my bound hands out so that she can untie the sloppy knot. "Thanks, ladies. I owe you."

"Nonsense," says Antoinette. "It is the least we can do after what you have done for us. Swinging me free from the Paris Temple —"

"— and whisking me away from the Ten Bells before that trasseno showed up and tried to hire me," Mary Jane adds, maternally brushing dirt off my shoulders. "You held a candle to the devil in a new way."

I pretend annoyance. "Would you mind speaking English for once, M.J.? Our Highness is more understandable, even with that crazy Austrian accent."

"This *is* English, Yank."

"Hardy har har."

Her Majesty looks at her Chopard Super Ice Cube wristwatch. "Let us make haste. Poor Elizabeth Short, the Black Dahlia, needs our aid not very far but quite a few years from here. Then we must be off to that scared communist town in the Guyana jungle. Then to the New Reich Chancellery and then to —"

Mary Jane interrupts and rolls her eyes. "And then and then and then . . ."

I stand and four lady hands help me rise from the streamer trunk. The queen and the whore free me from my premature grave.

BENEDICTION

Buried Alive — *Alive*!

Re-sight!

I see now, after weeps until numb,
illness, starvation, plagues, rape.
There's peace.

We disinter Humanity's corpse and
open its chest to find that peace —
a living peace — abides despite.

Seen, if we look with new eyes.

Who would have thought? A peace —
in this: this burning house, this tearful
valley. Hidden out in the open, like
Poe's purloined letter, asserting: "No,
death. Yes, life." Yes, life. No death.

The bells peal "sanctuary!"
"God isn't isn't!"

Go tell it on the mountain, scoop the
story before it's spun, before the demons
revise it to "All's lost," "No news is good
news," "Que sera sera," "It is what it is."

Good King Wenceslas, Who You Are,
I find footing in your deep path: infant
feet in mastodon prints, flesh saved by wine.
Skulls scare fruitlessly outside the door of Life.

The Abyss turns tail and runs.
Nobody is nobody!

Guillotines can't chop poets' necks,
human life teems among the tombs.
Sire, you've found us though we run
and hide from you again and again.
A peace lives, seen by our new eyes.

Re-sight!

SELECTED SOURCES AND READING SUGGESTIONS

Beauty & Art by Elizabeth Prettejohn

The Nude by Kenneth Clarke

"Further Notes on Edgar Poe" and *Flowers of Evil* by Baudelaire (trans. Jonathan Mayne/Joanna Richardson)

The Lifeline and *The True Art of Painting* and interviews/letters by Magritte (trans. Richard Miller)

"Art" and "Love" by Ralph Waldo Emerson

On Art and Life and "The Relation of Art to Morals" by John Ruskin

The Sublime and Beautiful by Edmund Burke

The Doors of Perception and *Heaven and Hell* by Aldous Huxley

Concerning the Spiritual in Art by Wassily Kandinsky (trans. M.T.H. Sadler)

Thus Spake Zarathustra and *The Birth of Tragedy* by Nietzsche (trans. Thomas Common/Francis Golffing)

Edward Hopper: 1882–1967 Transformation of the Real by Rolf G. Renner

The Marriage of Heaven and Hell by William Blake

The Ethics of Psychoanalysis (1959–1960) by Jacques Lacan (trans. Dennis Porter)

"Visual Pleasure and Narrative Cinema" by Laura Mulvey

The Romantic Manifesto by Ayn Rand

The Origins of Totalitarian Democracy by J.L. Talmon

Juliette and *Justine* by Marquis de Sade (trans. Austryn Wainhouse)

Reflections on the Revolution in France by Edmund Burke

Marie Antoinette: The Journey by Antonia Fraser

The 18th Brumaire of Napoleon Bonaparte by Karl Marx

Citizens: A Chronicle of the French Revolution by Simon Schama

The Old Regime and the French Revolution by Alexis de Tocqueville (trans. Stuart Gilbert)

Age of the French Revolution by Claude Manceron (trans. Nancy Amphoux)

On Revolution and *On Violence* by Hannah Arendt

Rules for Radicals by Saul Alinsky

The Dangers of American Liberty by Fisher Ames

Les Miserables, *The Last Day of a Condemned Man* and *The Hunchback of Notre Dame* by Victor Hugo (trans. Lee Fahnestock and Norman MacAfee/Arabella Ward/Walter J. Cobb)

Confessions and *The Social Contract* by Jean-Jacques Rousseau (trans. J.M. Cohen/G.D.H. Cole)

The Scarlet Pimpernel by Baroness Orczy

"Harriet Shelley: Wife of the Poet" by John Lauritsen

Shadow and Act and *Invisible Man* by Ralph Ellison

Moby-Dick by Herman Melville

Black Boy by Richard Wright

How Should We Then Live? and *Escape From Reason* by Francis A. Schaeffer

The Abolition of Man and *A Grief Observed* by C.S. Lewis

Notes from Underground and *Devils* by Dostoyevsky (trans. Mirra Ginsburg/Michael R. Katz)

Walden Two by B.F. Skinner

The New Deal edited by David E. Hamilton

Pensees by Blaise Pascal (trans. A.J. Krailsheimer)

The Mystery of Being by Gabriel Marcel (trans. G.S. Fraser)

Man in the Modern Age by Karl Jaspers (trans. Eden and Cedar Paul)

American Prometheus by Kai Bird and Martin J. Sherwin

Agents of Atrocity by Neil J. Mitchell

The Psychoanalysis of War by Franco Fornari (trans. Alenka Pfeifer)

Crowds and Power by Elias Canetti (trans. Carol Stewart)

The God of the Machine by Isabel Paterson

Deracination: Historicity, Hiroshima and the Tragic Imperative by Walter A. Davis

The Man Who Was Thursday and *The Everlasting Man* by G.K. Chesterton

Spiritual Writings and *Attack Upon "Christendom"* by Kierkegaard (trans. George Pattidon/Walter Lowrie)

God in Search of Man by Abraham Joshua Heschel

Hitler Youth by Michael H. Kater

The Survivor: An Anatomy of Life in the Death Camps by Terrence Des Pres

Hitler's Beneficiaries by Gotz Aly

Nazi Culture by George L. Mosse

The Last Days of the Romanovs by Helen Rappaport

The Conscience of the Revolution by Robert Vincent Daniels

Comrades! by Robert Service

Mao by Ross Terrill

Pol Pot: Anatomy of a Nightmare by Philip Short

For What Tomorrow . . . by Jacques Derrida and Elisabeth Roudinesco (trans. Jeff Fort)

I and Thou by Martin Buber (trans. Walter Kaufmann)

On the High Wire by Philippe Petit

The Lost Life of Eva Braun by Angela Lambert

Anais Nin by Deirdre Bair

Cyrano de Bergerac by Edmund Rostand (trans. Brian Hooker)

The Beauty Myth by Naomi Wolf

The Good, the Bad and the Barbie: A Doll's History and Her Impact on Us by Tanya Lee Stone

The Ethics of Ambiguity by Simone De Beauvoir

Soul On Ice by Eldridge Cleaver

The Ultimate Jack the Ripper Companion and *Jack the Ripper and the Whitechapel Murders* Stewart P. Evans and Keith Skinner

Jack the Ripper: The Final Solution by Stephen Knight

Jack the Ripper: The Final Chapter by Paul H. Feldman

The Waste Land by T.S. Eliot

Sharon Tate and the Manson Murders by Greg King

"Then It All Came Down" by Truman Capote

Charles Manson Now by Marlin Marynick

The Myth of Helter Skelter by Susan Atkins-Whitehouse

Helter Skelter by Vincent Bugliosi (with Curt Gentry)

Restless Souls by Alisa Statman (with Brie Tate)

EXTRACTS

"Who can analyze the nameless charm which glances from one and another face and form?" — Emerson

"I suppose there is a horrible kink in one's disposition that tends always to kick against anything that is too right or too perfect." — Agatha Christie

"[I]n a faire body, I do seldom suspect a disproportioned minde, and as seldom hope for a good, in a deformed." — John Donne

"[W]hoever refuses to obey the general will shall be compelled to do so by the whole body. This means nothing less than that he will be forced to be free." — Rousseau

"[W]ork is going on which boldly attacks the pillars which men have set up. There we find other professional men of learning who test matter again and again . . . and who finally cast doubt on that very matter which was yesterday the foundation of everything . . ." — Kandinsky

"If a revolution find the citizens lambs, it will soon make them carnivorous, if not cannibals." — Fisher Ames

"As for that liberty which you love to excess, you have only considered its advantages. You have not taken into account the disorders that come in liberty's wake." — Madame Elisabeth, Louis XVI's sister

"Ye preachers of equality, the tyrant-frenzy of impotence crieth thus in you for 'equality': your most secret tyrant-longings disguise themselves thus in virtue-words!" — Nietzsche

"Is he a poet? . . . An emancipator? Or a subjugator?" — Nietzsche

"Citizens, I declare to you that your progress is madness, that your humanity is a dream, that your revolution is a crime, that your republic is a monster . . . and I maintain it against all . . . even were you better judges of liberty, of equality, and fraternity than the knife of the guillotine!" — Gillenormand, *Les Miserables*

"They viciously snapped, not only at each other's disembowelments, but like flexible bows, bent round, and bit their own; till those entrails seemed swallowed over and over again by the same mouth . . ." — Ishmael on sharks, *Moby-Dick*

"The point to be stressed is that, when nature is made autonomous, it is destructive." — Francis Schaeffer

"Horror is the eloquent rejoinder to humanistic reassurance about the fundamental goodness of 'human nature.'" — Walter A. Davis

"[T]he head of the female veto separated from her fucking tart's neck." — Jacques Hebert on Antoinette

"My whole beaten brain seems as beheaded, and rolling on some stunning ground." — Ahab, *Moby-Dick*

"[H]e is as good as he is evil; he is as evil as he is good." — Susan Atkins on Charles Manson

"[T]here are two heads left . . . That is, one of the heads is mine, and the other — that monster's. So choose: me or the monster?" — Dmitri, *The Brothers Karamazov*

"Think of the bewilderment of trying to get into a room in which you already are! Think of the absurdity of asking to be put in! . . . [W]e *are* in . . ." — Watchman Nee

"In the vilest and most arrant rubbish I would have managed to discern the lofty and the beautiful." — *Notes from Underground*

"Plunge down to find the place where nothing breathes, into the blackness that is hidden inside it. Keep going until you reach the other side of the light. It is a dazzling clarity, a clamorous splendor . . . " — Philippe Petit

"In the midst of the foulest decay and putrid savagery, this spark speaks to you of beauty, of human warmth and kindness, of goodness, of greatness, of heroism, of martyrdom, and it speaks to you of love." — Eldridge Cleaver

BIOGRAPHICAL NOTE

David lives in Pittsburgh with his wife Marsha, and his children Kara-Zeal and Emerson Welles. He is the founder of *SubtleTea*.com and the author of *Abyssinia, Jill Rush* (Time Being Books, 2010).

OTHER POETRY AND SHORT FICTIONS AVAILABLE FROM TIME BEING BOOKS

Yakov Azriel

Beads for the Messiah's Bride: Poems on Leviticus
In the Shadow of a Burning Bush: Poems on Exodus
Swimming in Moses' Well: Poems on Numbers
Threads from a Coat of Many Colors: Poems on Genesis

Edward Boccia

No Matter How Good the Light Is: Poems by a Painter

Louis Daniel Brodsky

At Dock's End: Poems of Lake Nebagamon, Volume Two
At Shore's Border: Poems of Lake Nebagamon, Volume Three
At Water's Edge: Poems of Lake Nebagamon, Volume One
By Leaps and Bounds: Volume Two of *The Seasons of Youth*
The Capital Café: Poems of Redneck, U.S.A.
Catchin' the Drift o' the Draft *(short fictions)*
Combing Florida's Shores: Poems of Two Lifetimes
The Complete Poems of Louis Daniel Brodsky: Volumes One–Four
Dine-Rite: Breakfast Poems
Disappearing in Mississippi Latitudes: Volume Two of *A Mississippi Trilogy*
The Eleventh Lost Tribe: Poems of the Holocaust
Eying Widening Horizons: Volume Five of *The Seasons of Youth*
Falling from Heaven: Holocaust Poems of a Jew and a Gentile *(Brodsky and Heyen)*
Forever, for Now: Poems for a Later Love
Four and Twenty Blackbirds Soaring
Gestapo Crows: Holocaust Poems
Getting to Unknow the Neighbors *(short fictions)*
A Gleam in the Eye: Volume One of *The Seasons of Youth*
Hopgrassers and Flutterbies: Volume Four of *The Seasons of Youth*
Just Ours: Love Passages with Linda, Volume One
Leaky Tubs *(short fictions)*
Mississippi Vistas: Volume One of *A Mississippi Trilogy*
Mistress Mississippi: Volume Three of *A Mississippi Trilogy*
Nuts to You! *(short fictions)*
Once upon a Small-Town Time: Poems of America's Heartland
Our Time: Love Passages with Linda, Volume Two
Paper-Whites for Lady Jane: Poems of a Midlife Love Affair
Peddler on the Road: Days in the Life of Willy Sypher
Pigskinizations *(short fictions)*
Rabbi Auschwitz: Poems of the Shoah
Rated Xmas *(short fictions)*
Saul and Charlotte: Poems Commemorating a Father and Mother

Louis Daniel Brodsky *(continued)*

Seizing the Sun and Moon: Volume Three of *The Seasons of Youth*

Shadow War: A Poetic Chronicle of September 11 and Beyond, Volumes One–Five

Showdown with a Cactus: Poems Chronicling the Prickly Struggle Between the Forces of Dubya-ness and Enlightenment, 2003–2006

Still Wandering in the Wilderness: Poems of the Jewish Diaspora

The Swastika Clock: Holocaust Poems

This Here's a Merica *(short fictions)*

The Thorough Earth

Three Early Books of Poems by Louis Daniel Brodsky, 1967–1969: *The Easy Philosopher*, *"A Hard Coming of It" and Other Poems*, and *The Foul Rag-and-Bone Shop*

Toward the Torah, Soaring: Poems of the Renascence of Faith

A Transcendental Almanac: Poems of Nature

Unser Kampf: Poems of the Final Solution

Voice Within the Void: Poems of *Homo supinus*

With One Foot in the Butterfly Farm *(short fictions)*

The World Waiting to Be: Poems About the Creative Process

Yellow Bricks *(short fictions)*

You Can't Go Back, Exactly

Harry James Cargas *(editor)*

Telling the Tale: A Tribute to Elie Wiesel on the Occasion of His 65th Birthday — Essays, Reflections, and Poems

Judith Chalmer

Out of History's Junk Jar: Poems of a Mixed Inheritance

Gerald Early

How the War in the Streets Is Won: Poems on the Quest of Love and Faith

Gary Fincke

Blood Ties: Working-Class Poems

Reviving the Dead

Charles Adès Fishman

Blood to Remember: American Poets on the Holocaust *(editor)*

Chopin's Piano

In the Path of Lightning

CB Follett

Hold and Release

One Bird Falling

Albert Goldbarth

A Lineage of Ragpickers, Songpluckers, Elegiasts & Jewelers: Selected
  Poems of Jewish Family Life, 1973–1995

Robert Hamblin

Crossroads: Poems of a Mississippi Childhood
From the Ground Up: Poems of One Southerner's Passage to Adulthood
Keeping Score: Sports Poems for Every Season

David Herrle

Abyssinia, Jill Rush

William Heyen

Erika: Poems of the Holocaust
Falling from Heaven: Holocaust Poems of a Jew and a Gentile *(Brodsky and Heyen)*
The Host: Selected Poems, 1965–1990
Pterodactyl Rose: Poems of Ecology
Ribbons: The Gulf War — A Poem

Ted Hirschfield

German Requiem: Poems of the War and the Atonement of a Third Reich Child

Virginia V. James Hlavsa

Waking October Leaves: Reanimations by a Small-Town Girl

Rodger Kamenetz

The Missing Jew: New and Selected Poems
Stuck: Poems Midlife

Norbert Krapf

Blue-Eyed Grass: Poems of Germany
Looking for God's Country
Somewhere in Southern Indiana: Poems of Midwestern Origins

Adrian C. Louis

Blood Thirsty Savages

Leo Luke Marcello

Nothing Grows in One Place Forever: Poems of a Sicilian American

866-840-4334
HTTP://WWW.TIMEBEING.COM

Gardner McFall
The Pilot's Daughter
Russian Tortoise

Joseph Meredith
Hunter's Moon: Poems from Boyhood to Manhood
Inclinations of the Heart

Ben Milder
From Adolescence to Senescence: A Life in Light Verse
The Good Book Also Says . . . : Numerous Humorous Poems Inspired by
    the New Testament
The Good Book Says . . . : Light Verse to Illuminate the Old Testament
Love Is Funny, Love Is Sad
What's So Funny About the Golden Years
The Zoo You Never Gnu: A Mad Menagerie of Bizarre Beasts and Birds

Charles Muñoz
Fragments of a Myth: Modern Poems on Ancient Themes

Brenda Marie Osbey
History and Other Poems

Micheal O'Siadhail
The Gossamer Wall: Poems in Witness to the Holocaust

Charles Rammelkamp
Fūsen Bakudan: Poems of Altruism and Tragedy in Wartime

Judith Sarah Schmidt
Longing for the Blessing: Midrashic Voices from Toldot

Joseph Stanton
A Field Guide to the Wildlife of Suburban O'ahu
Imaginary Museum: Poems on Art

Susan Terris
Contrariwise